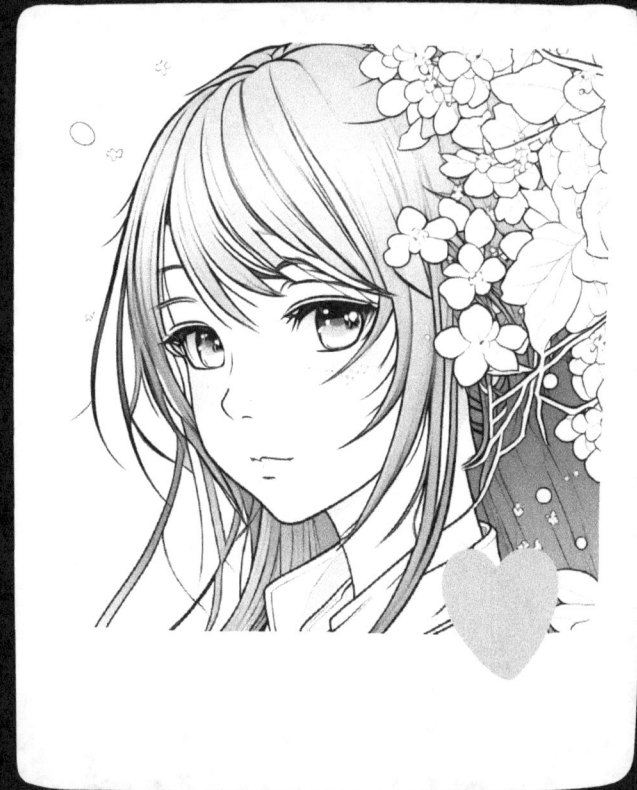

塗り絵 SUPER KAWAII PRINCESSES

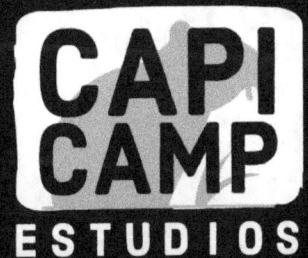

CAPI CAMP

ESTUDIOS

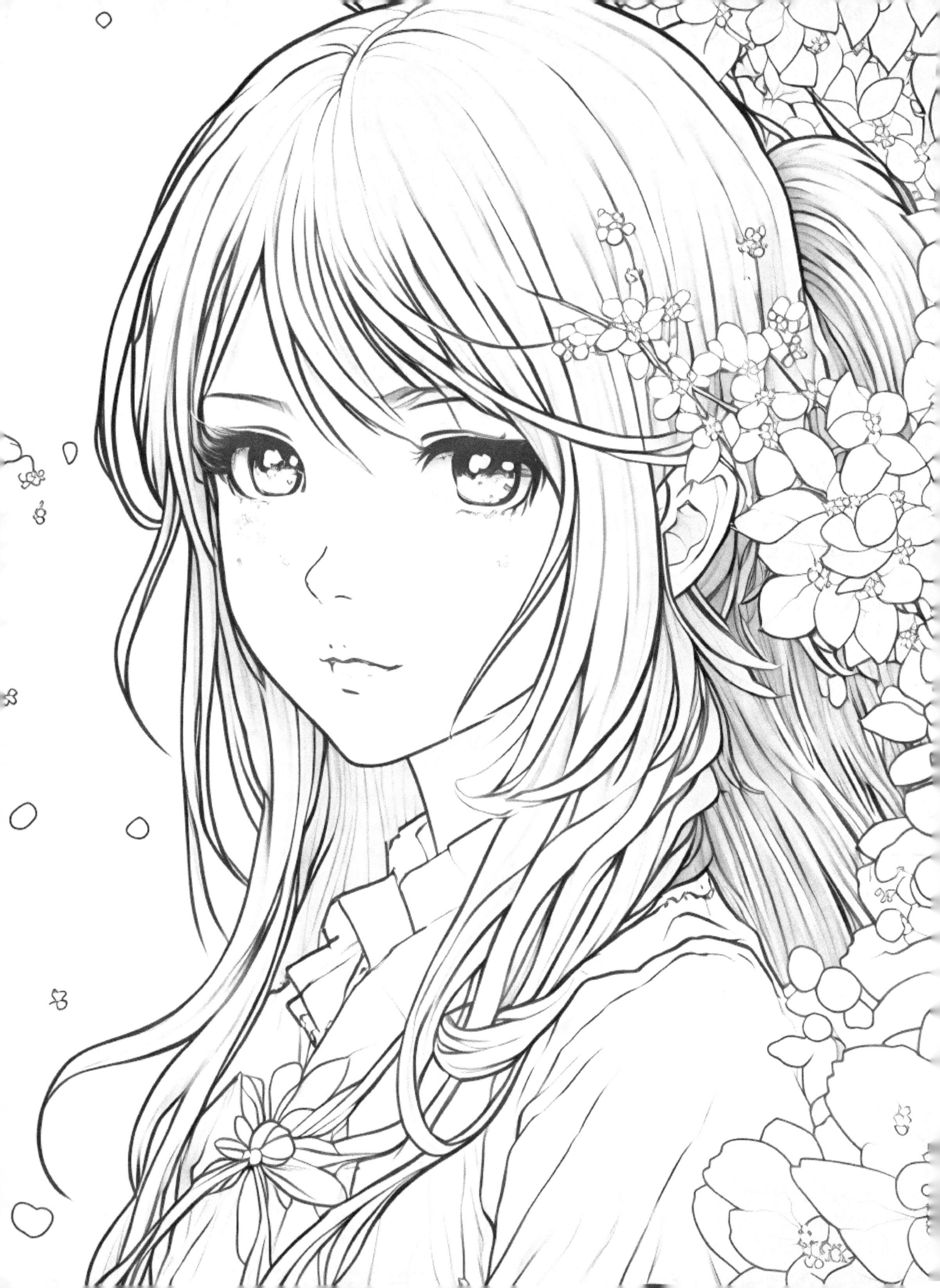

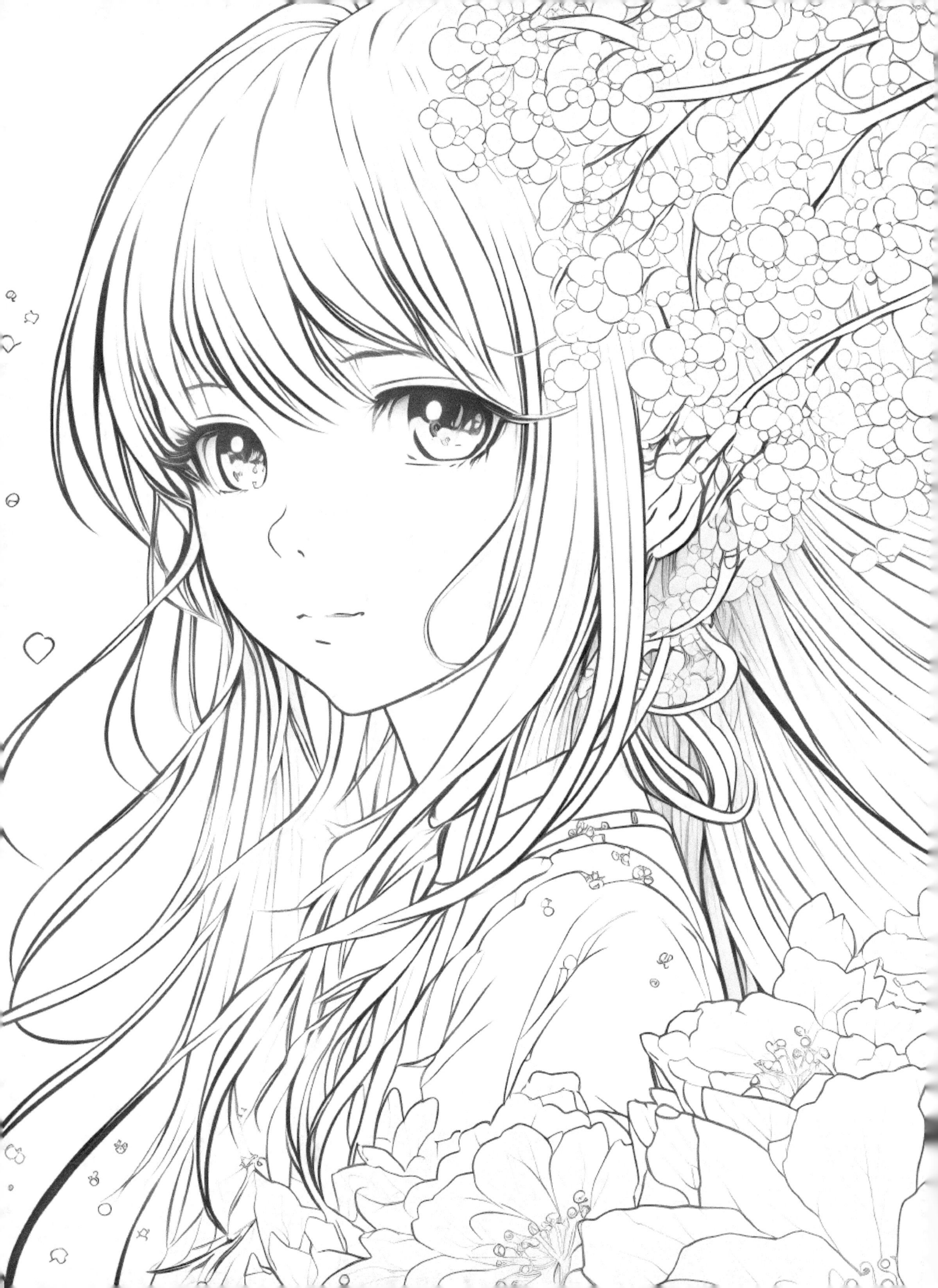

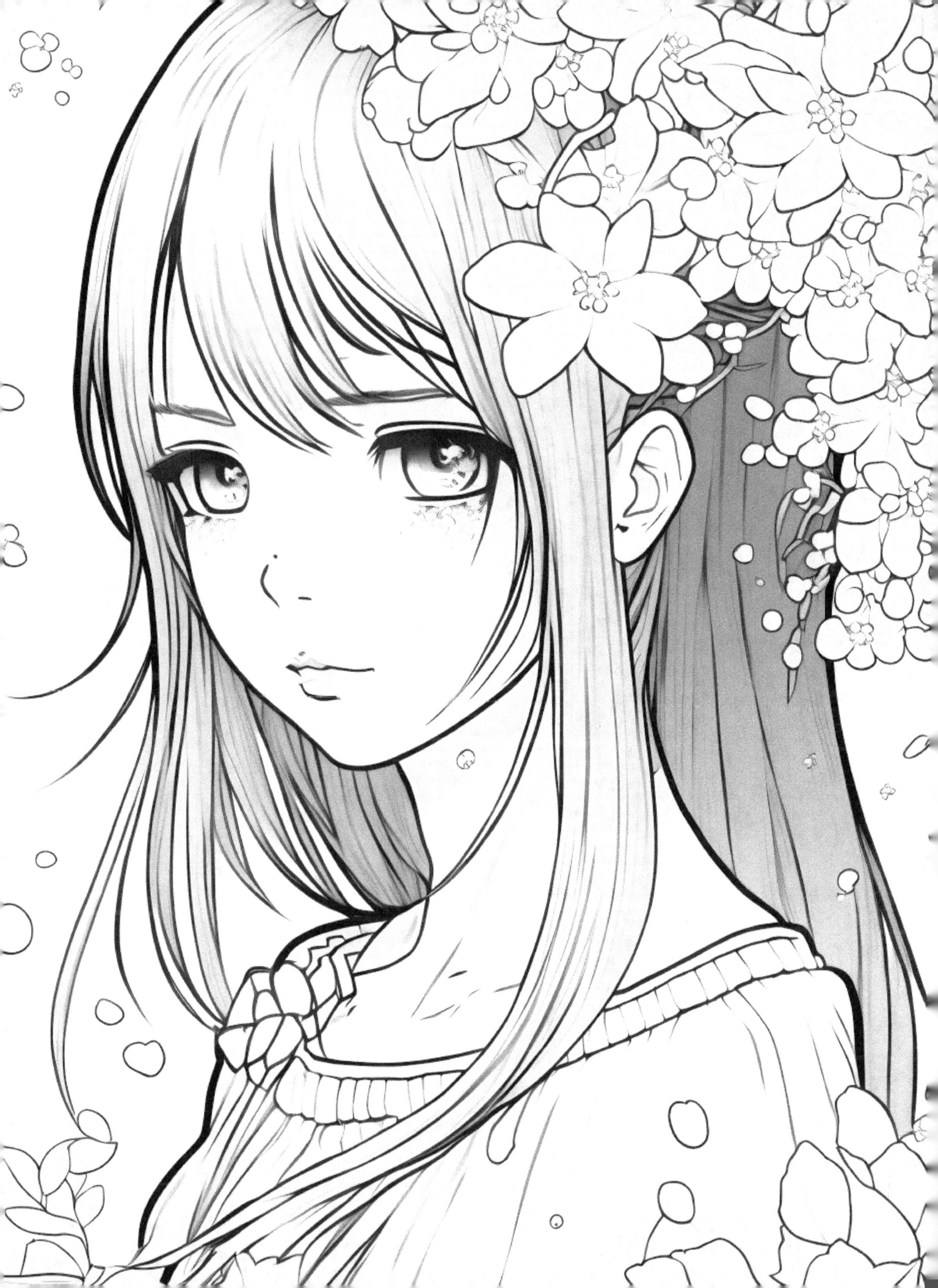

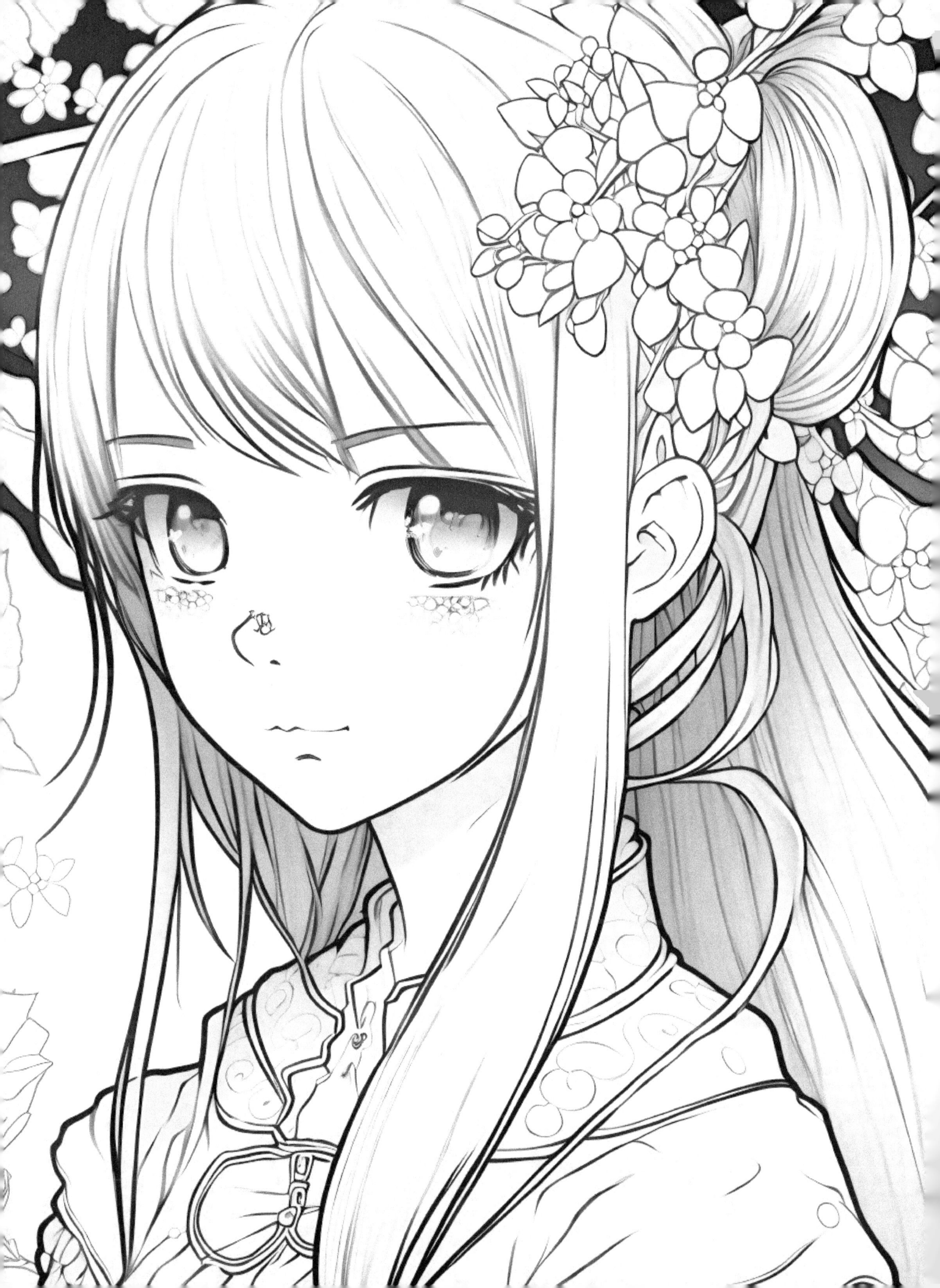

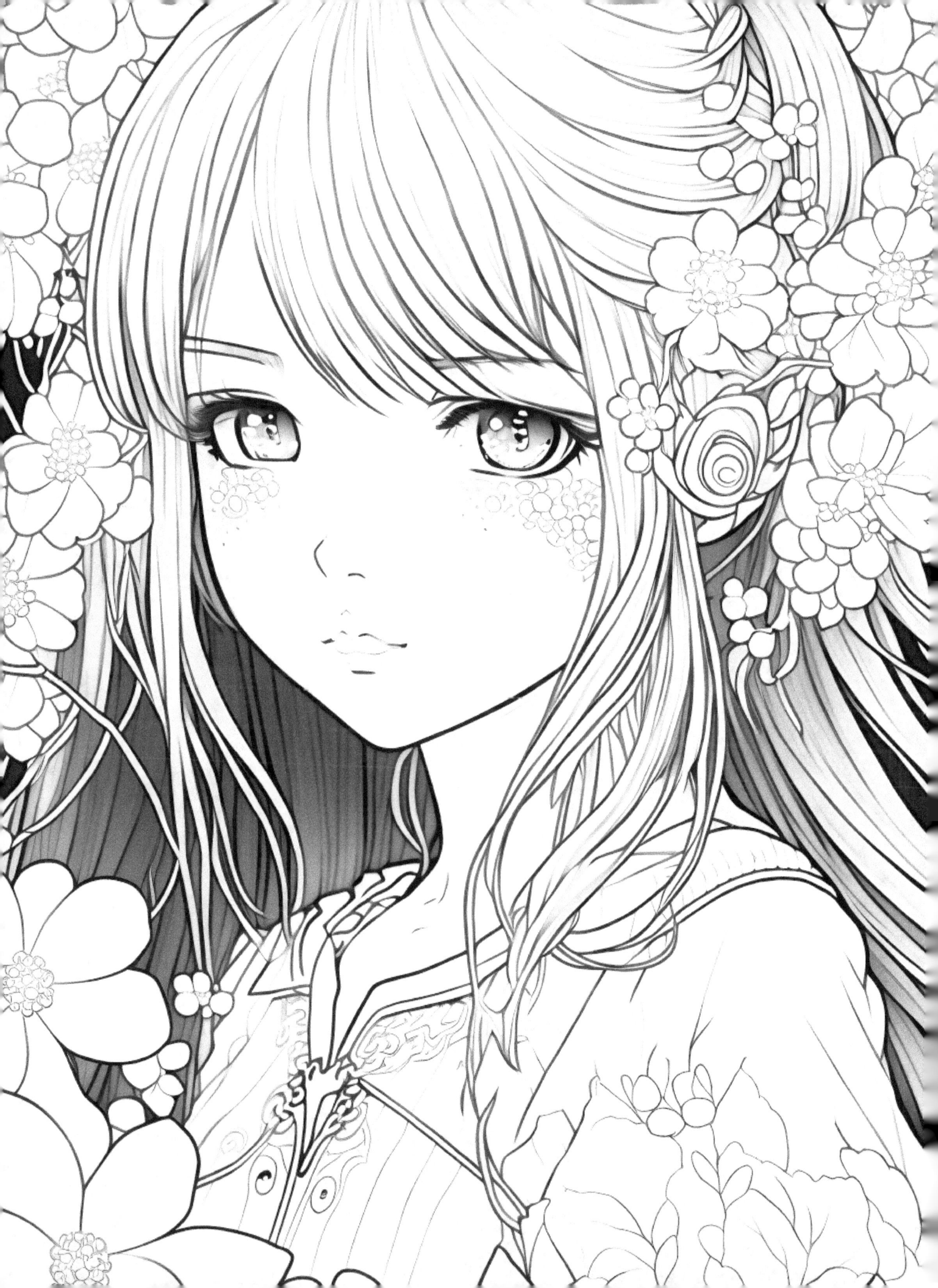

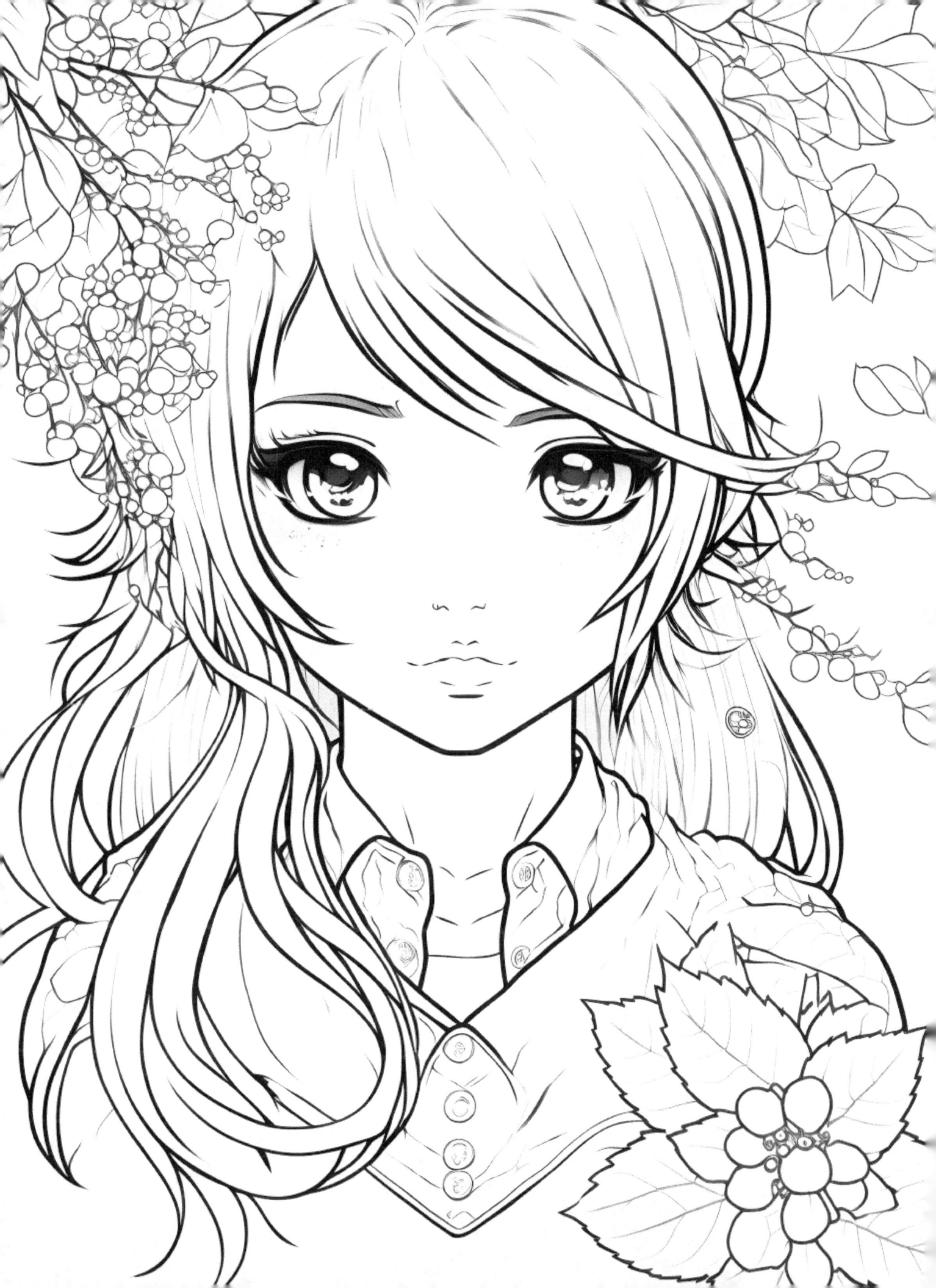

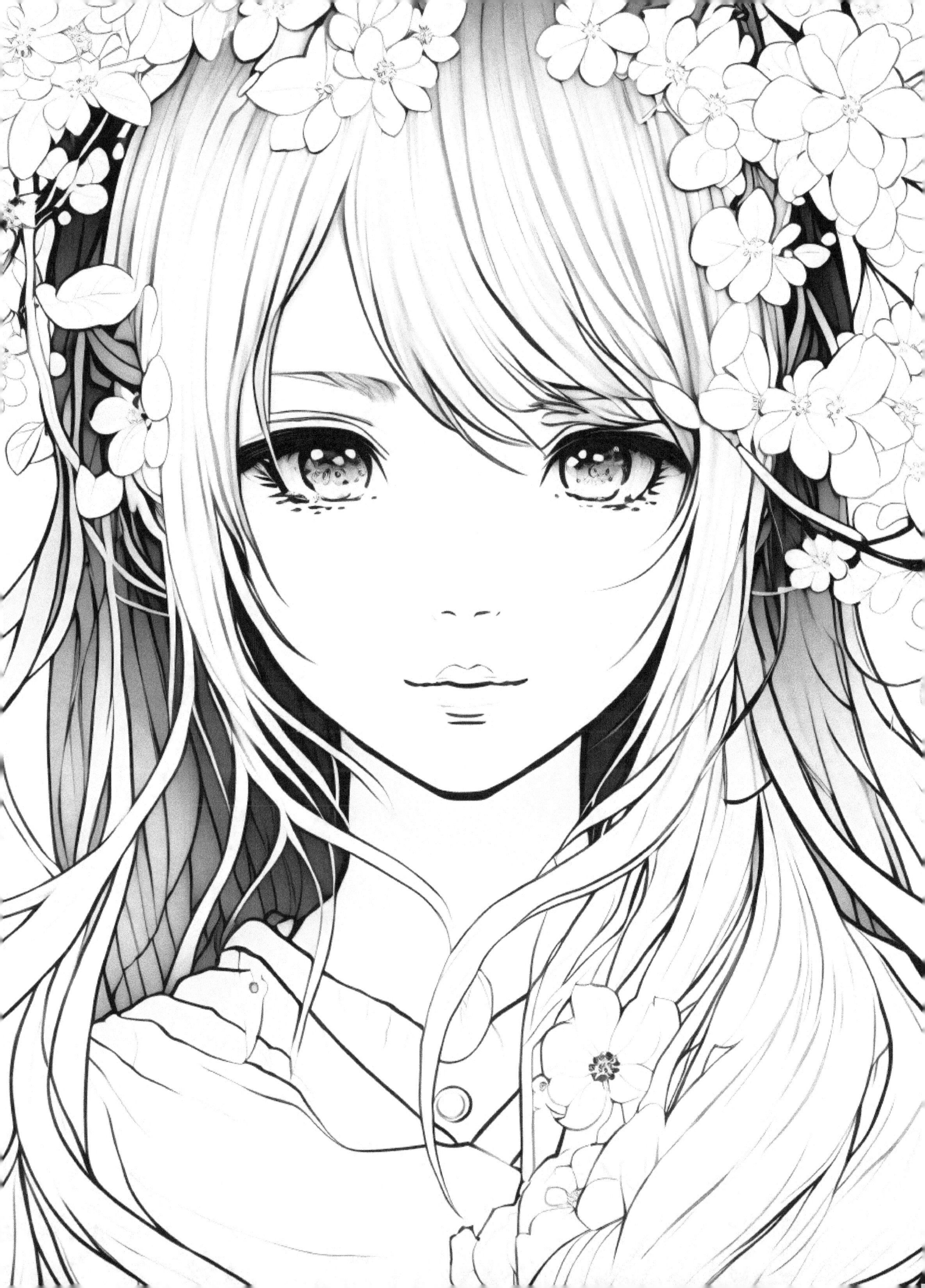

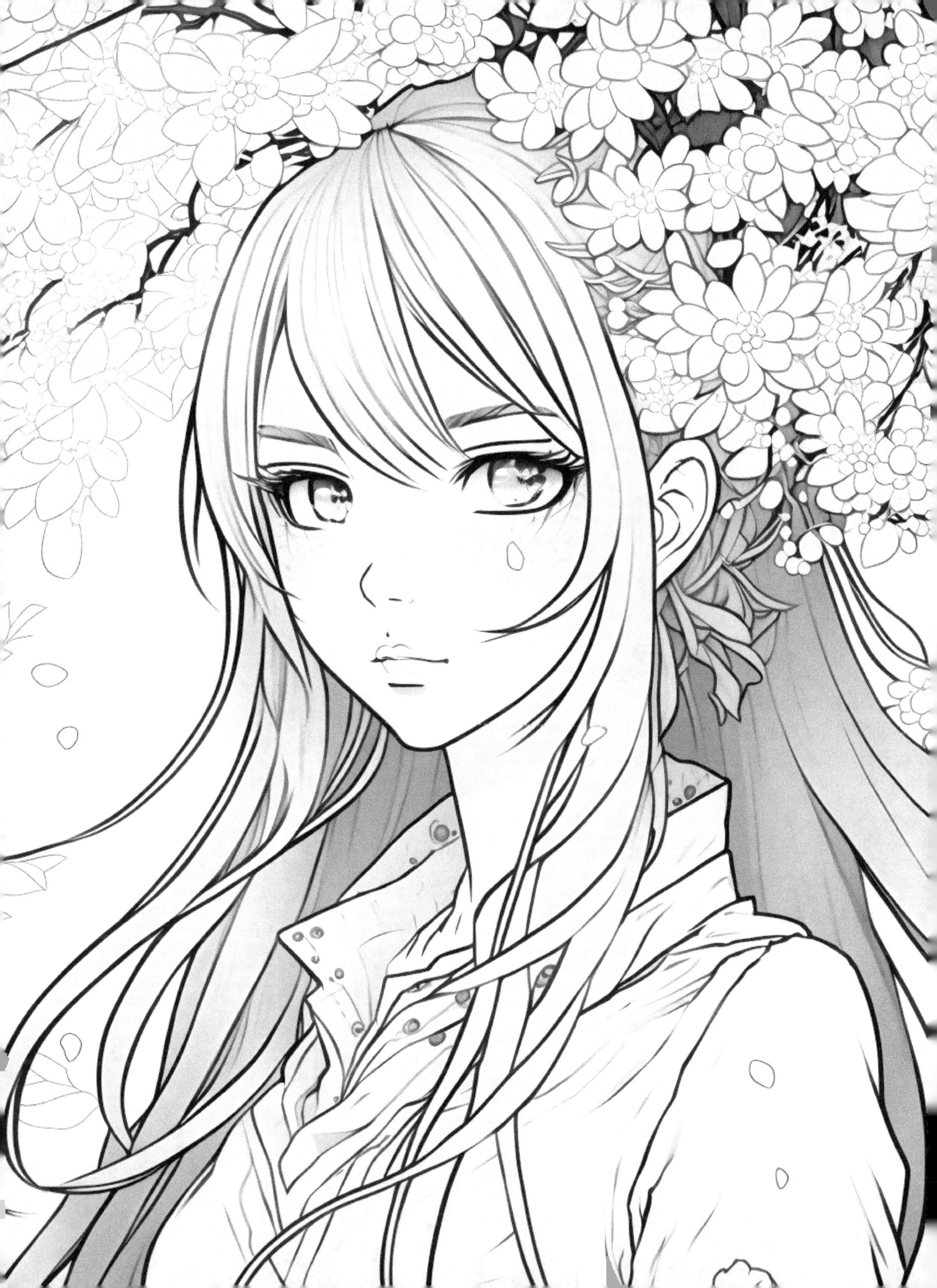

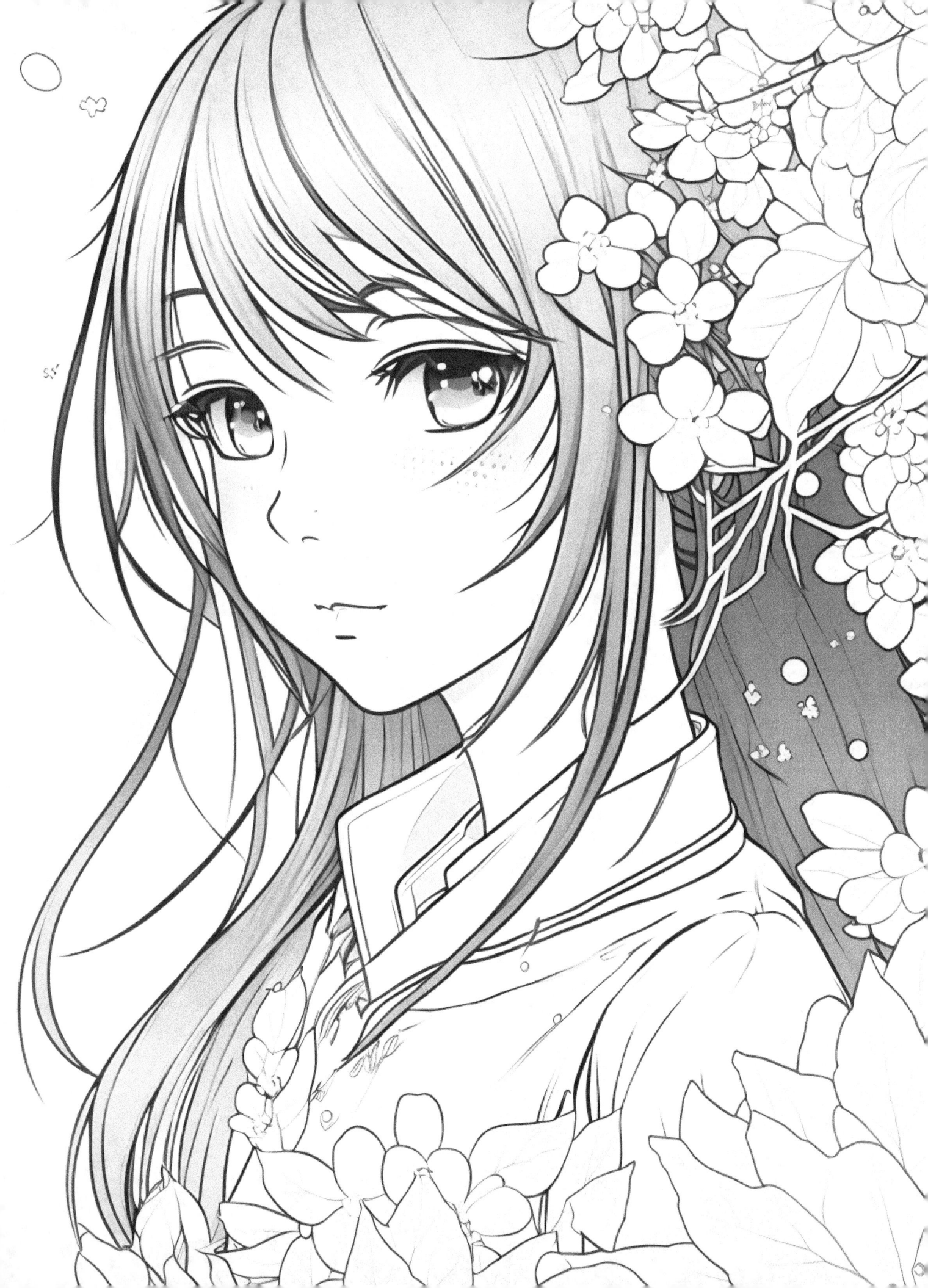

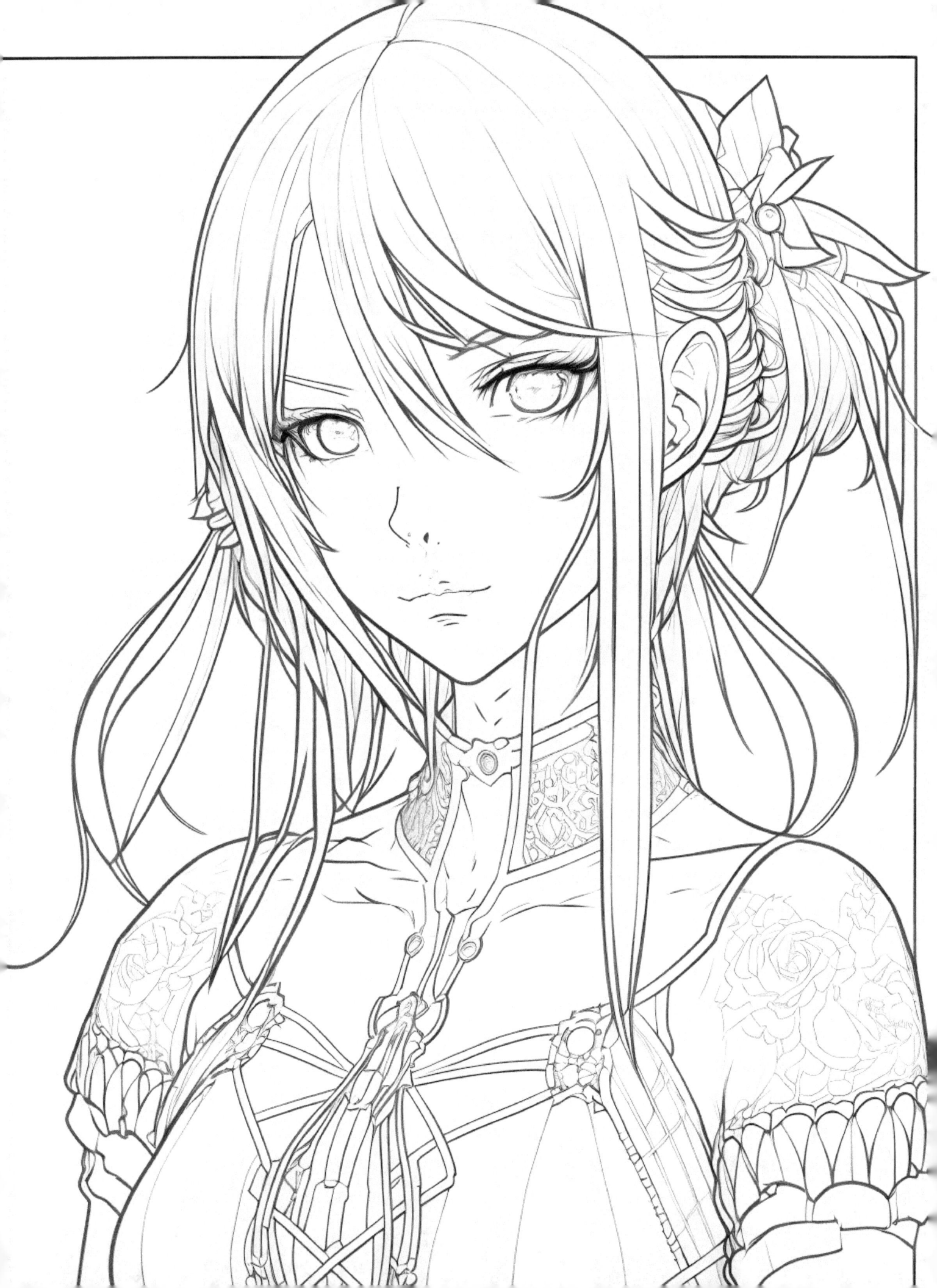

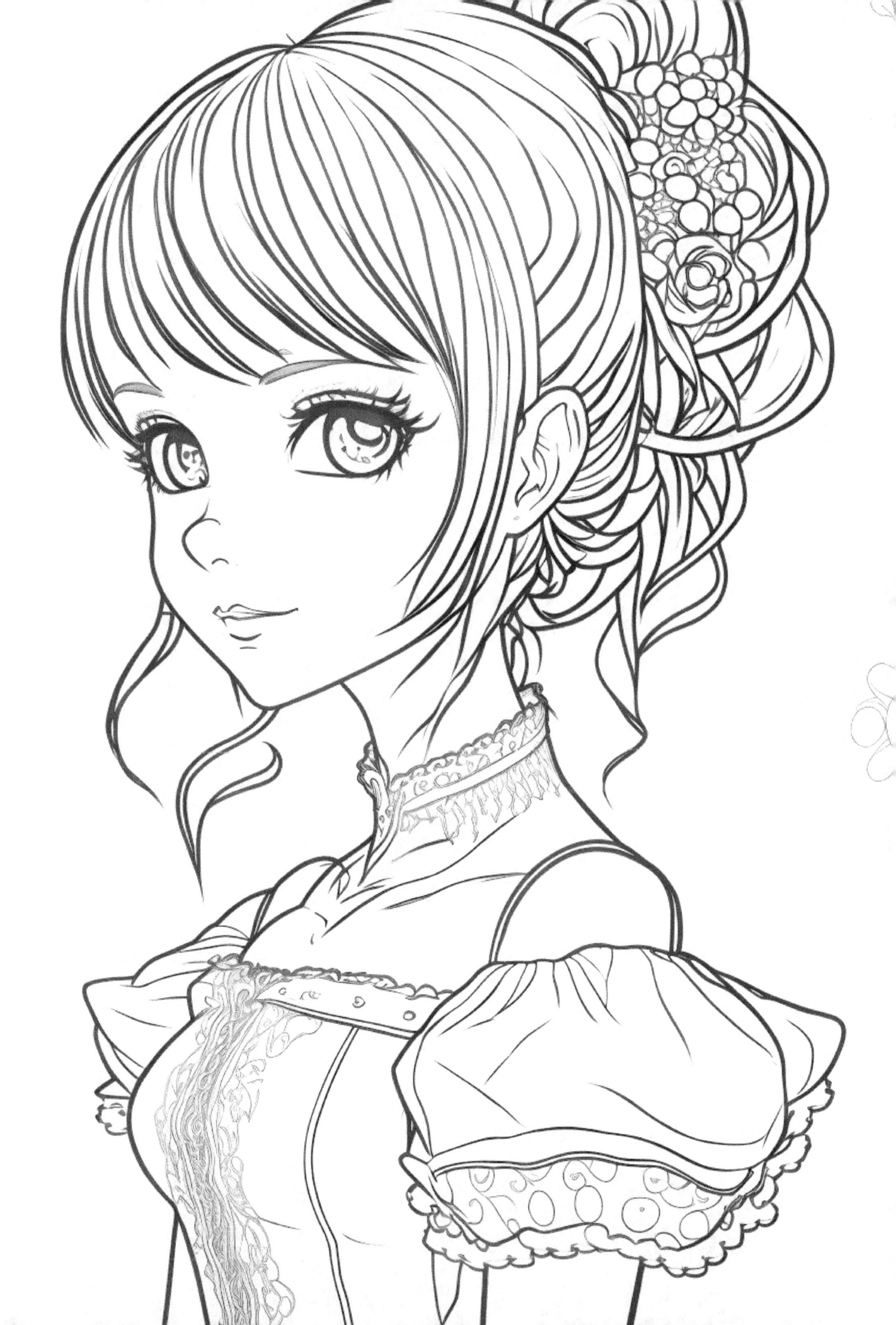

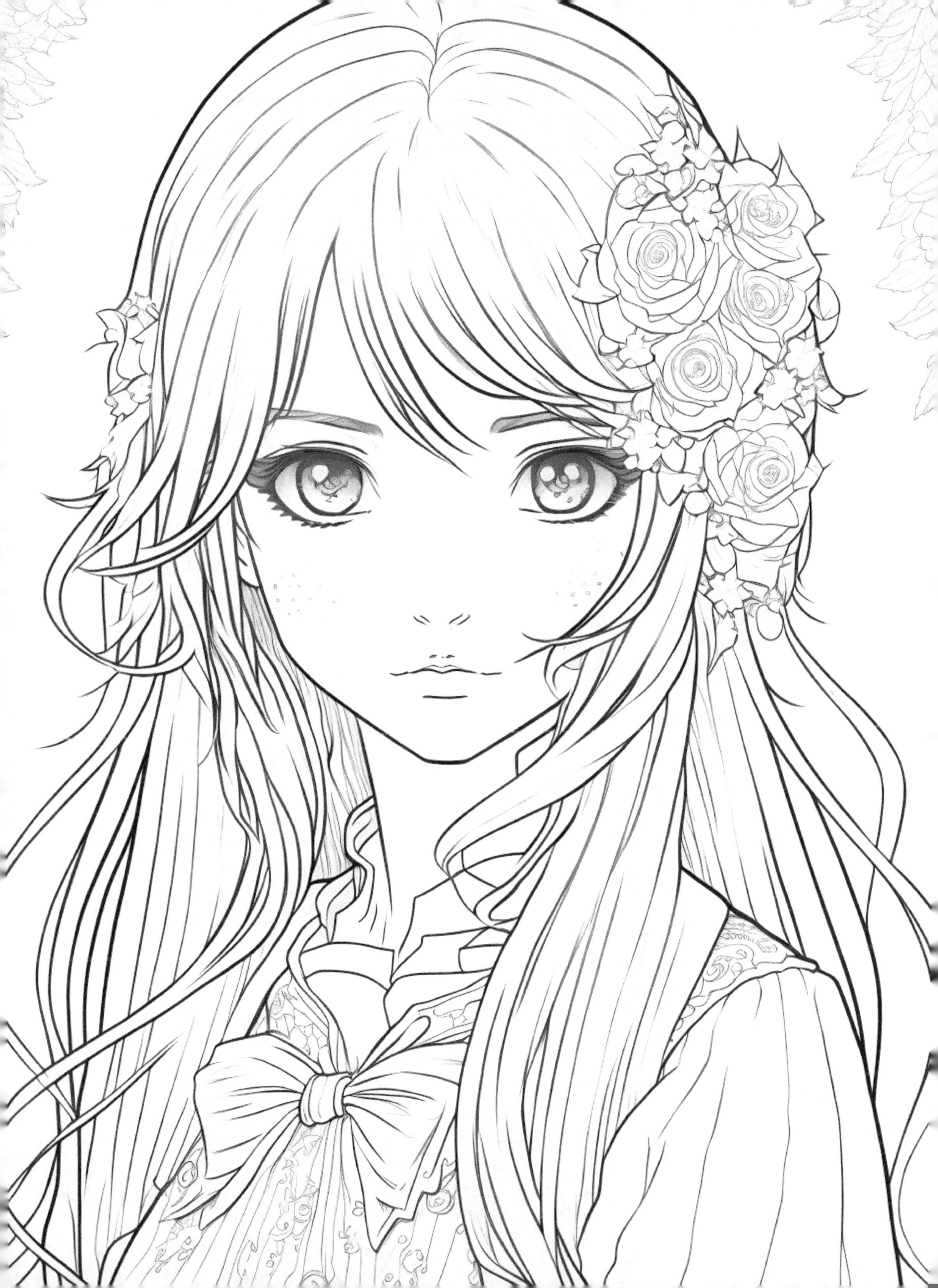

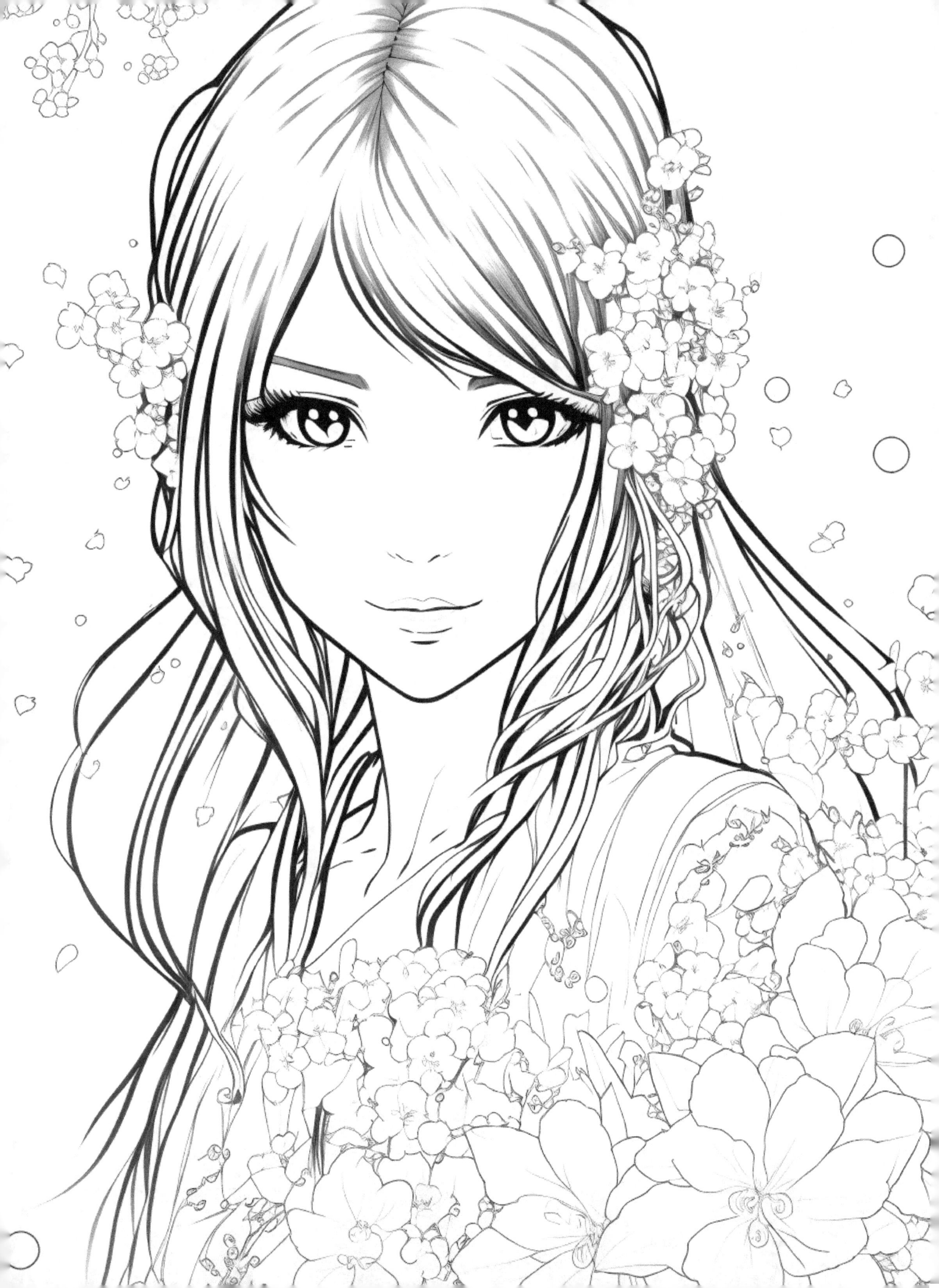

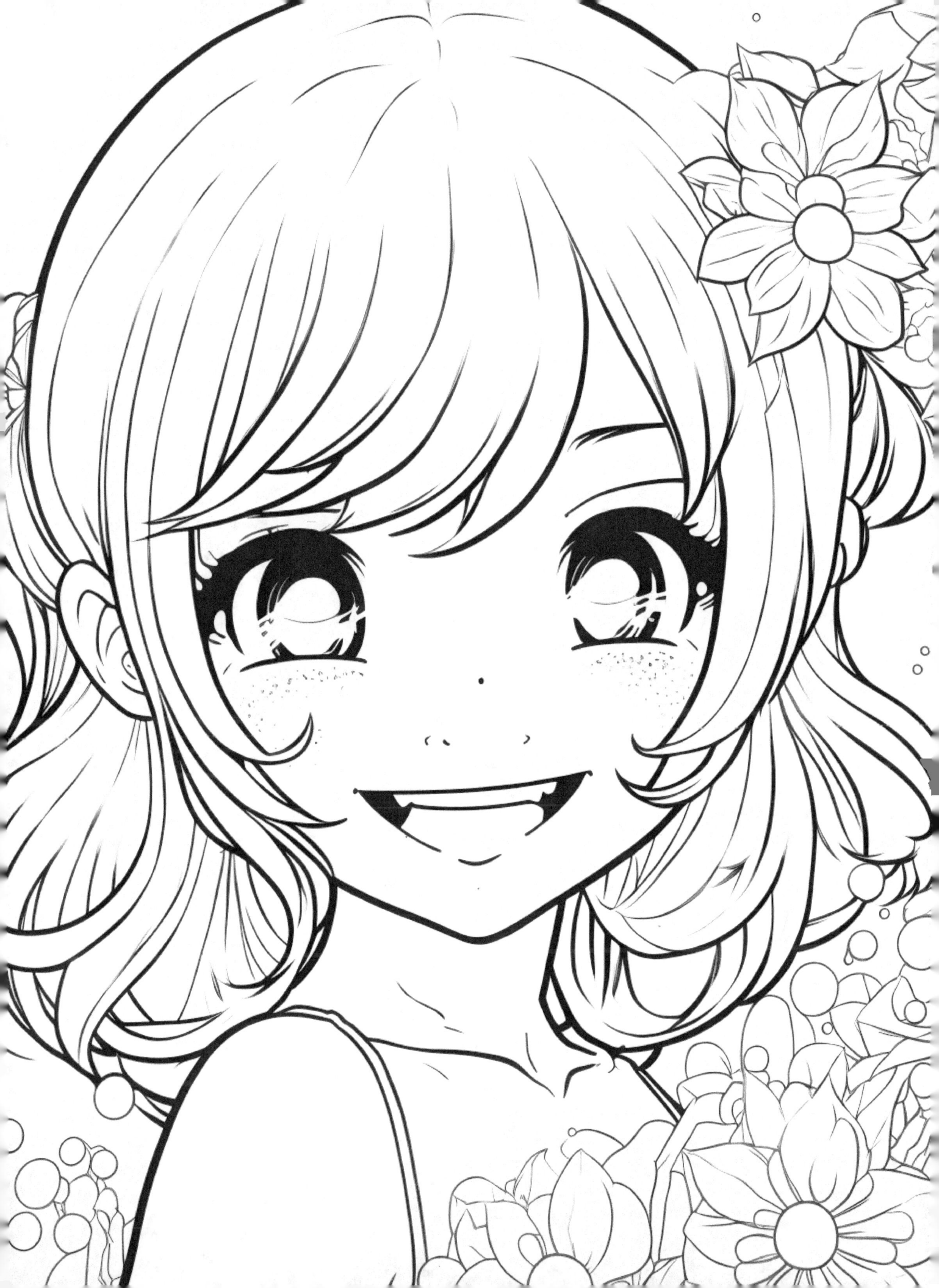

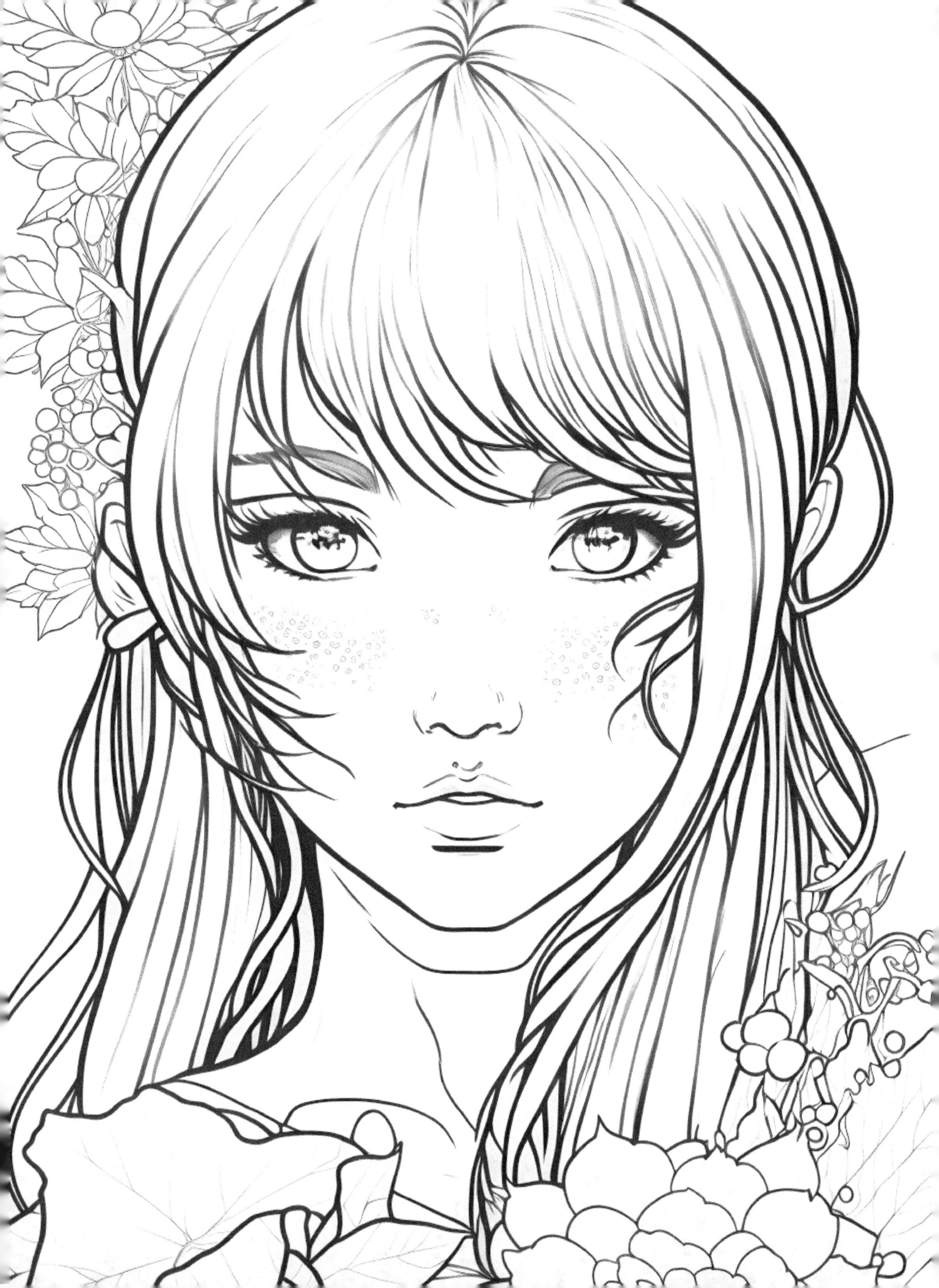

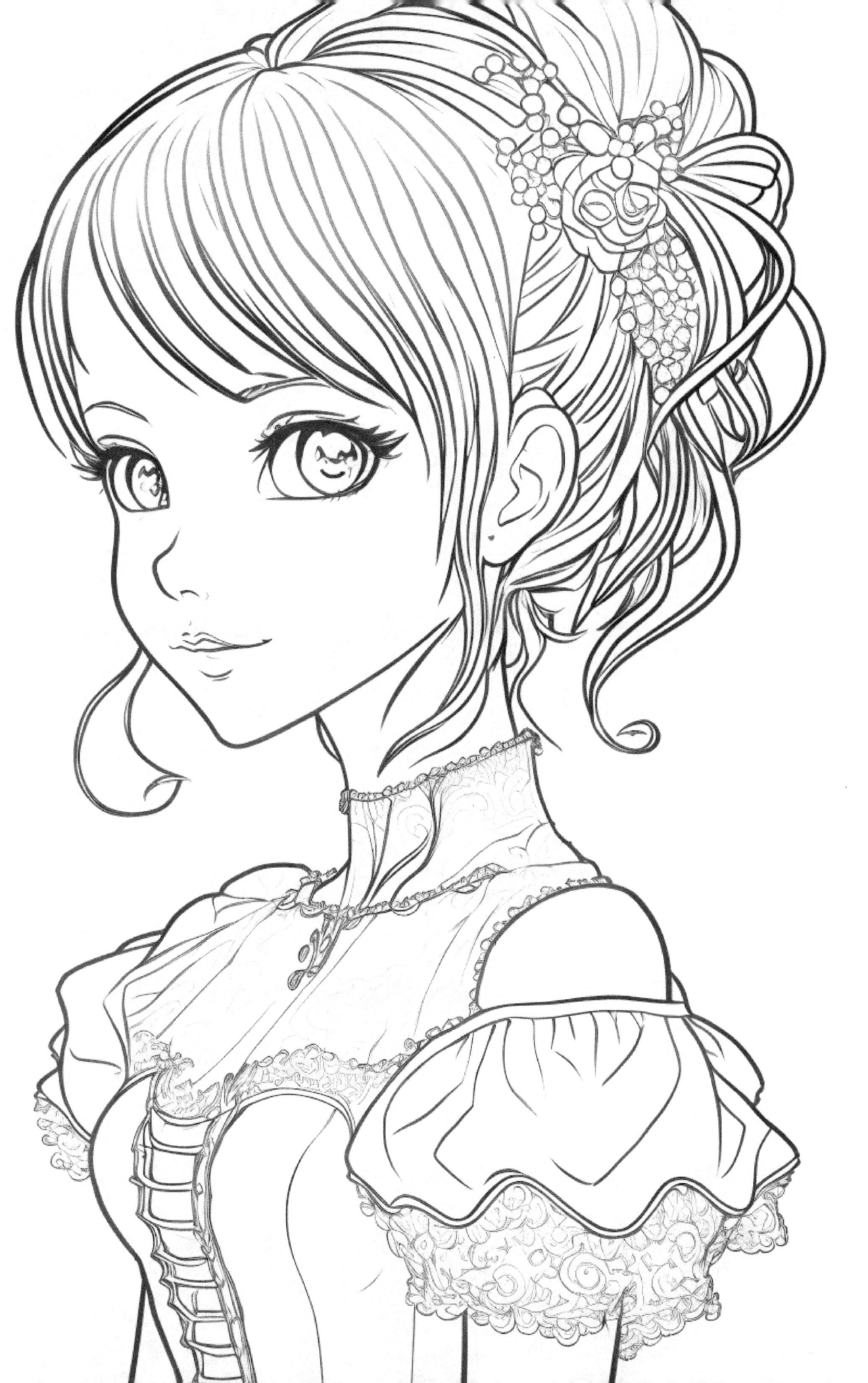

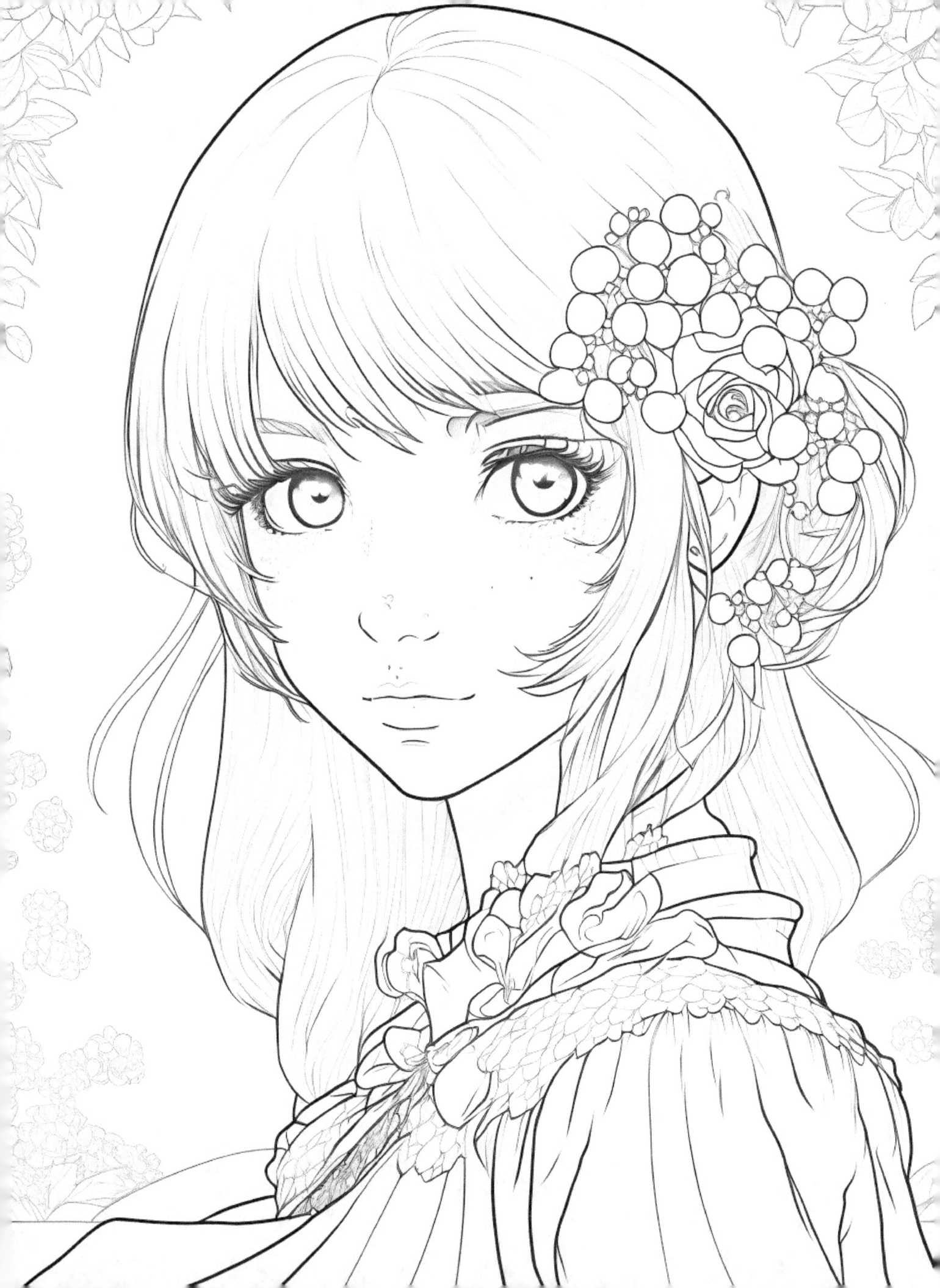

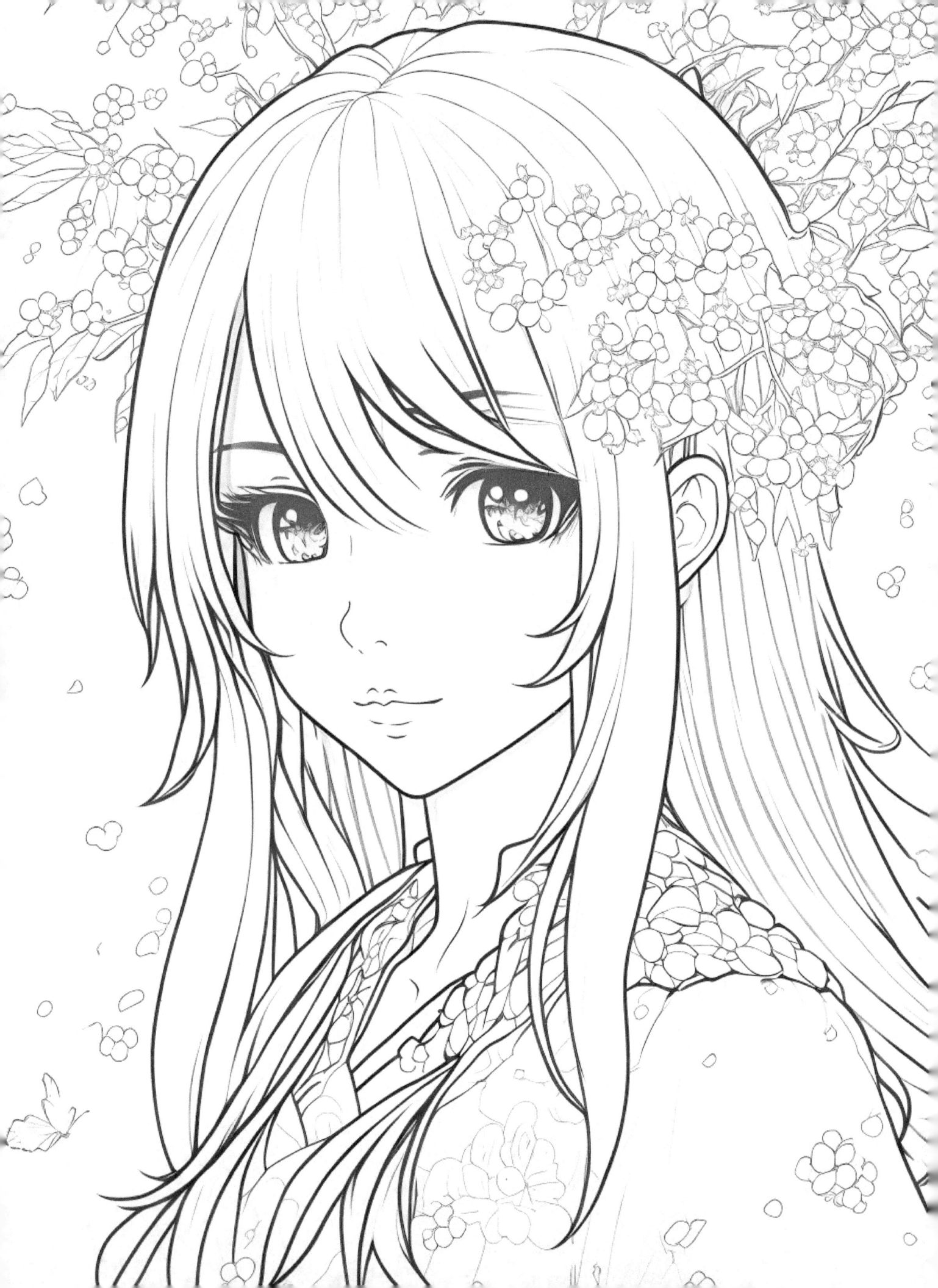

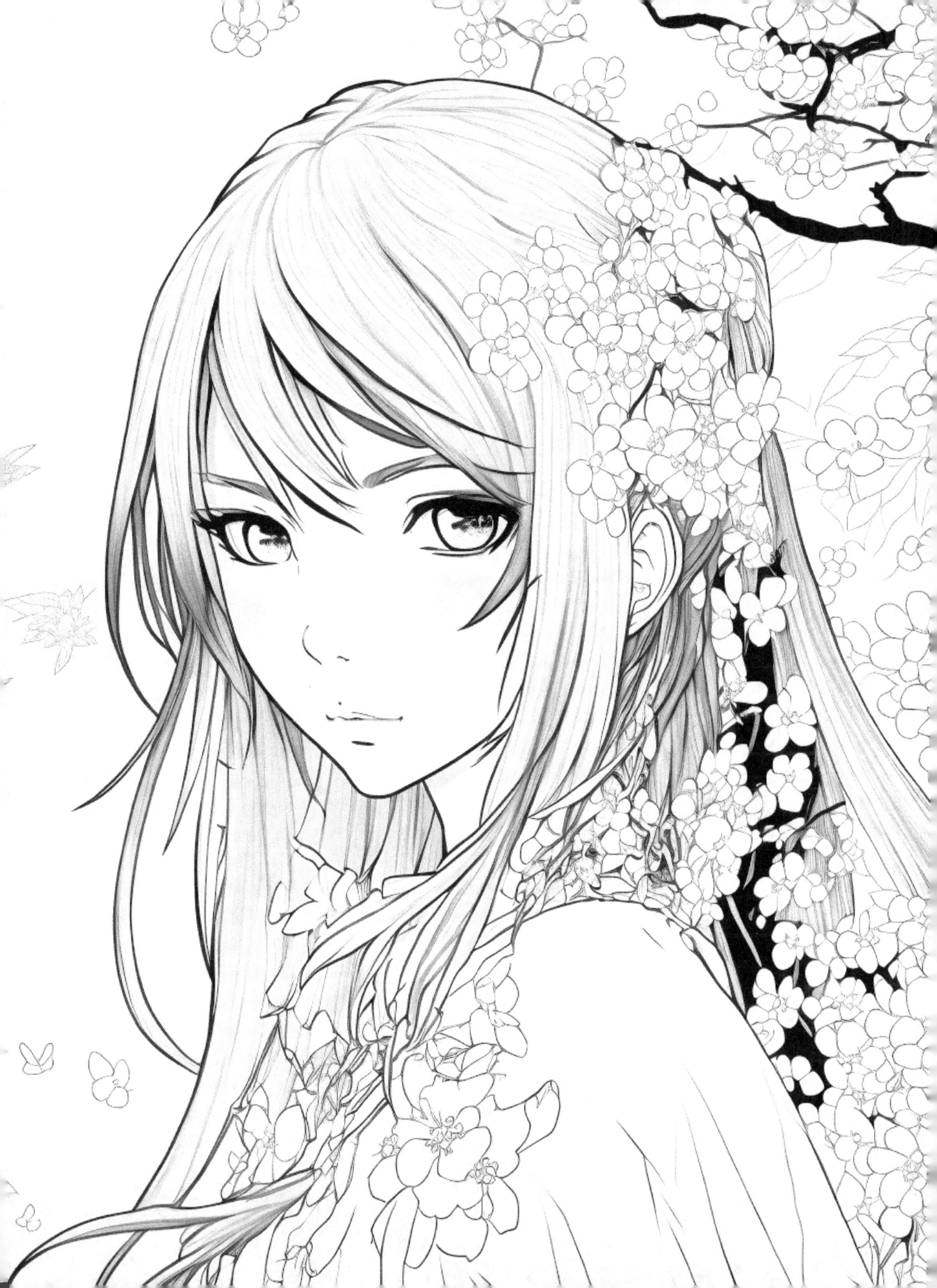

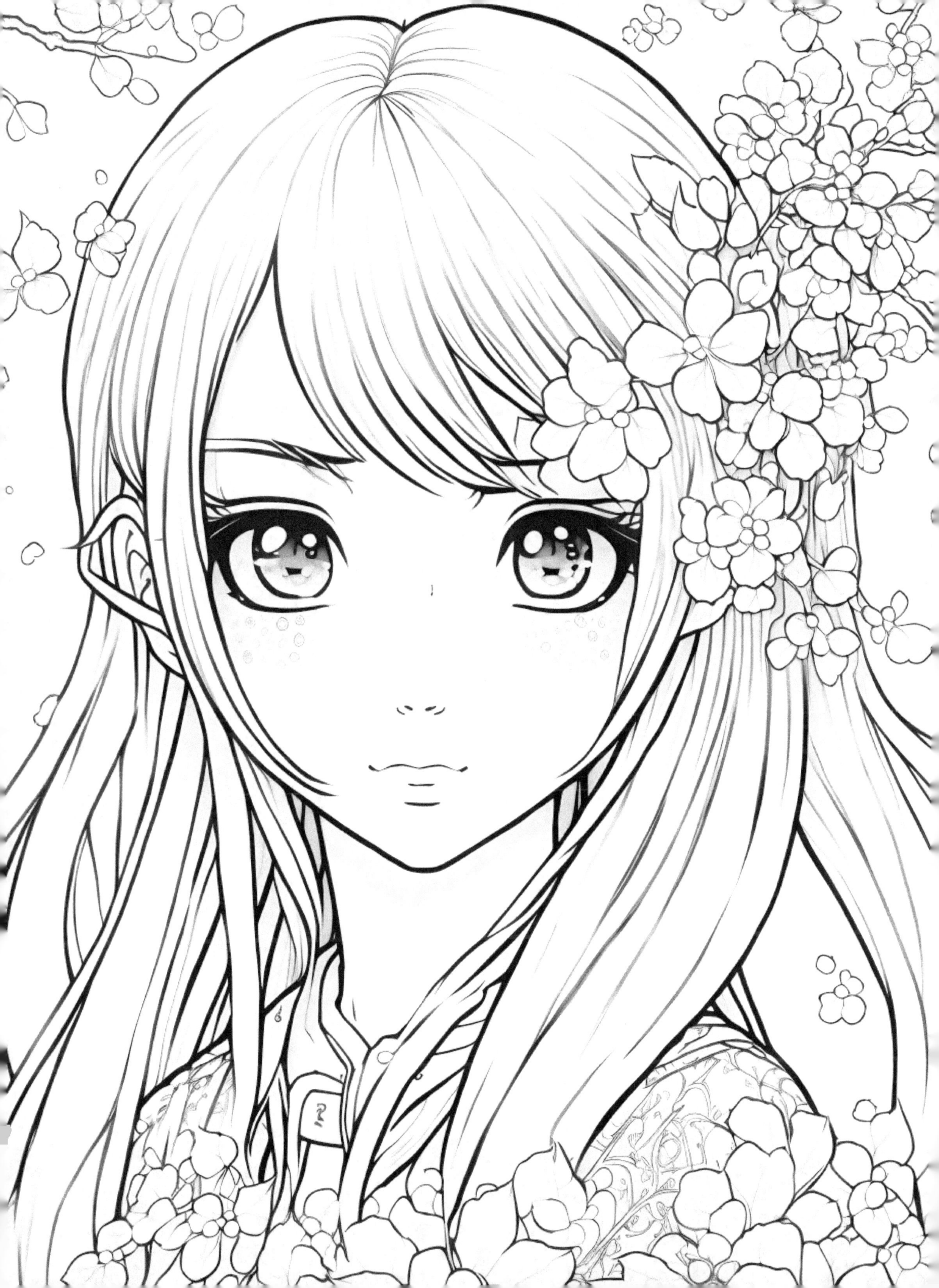

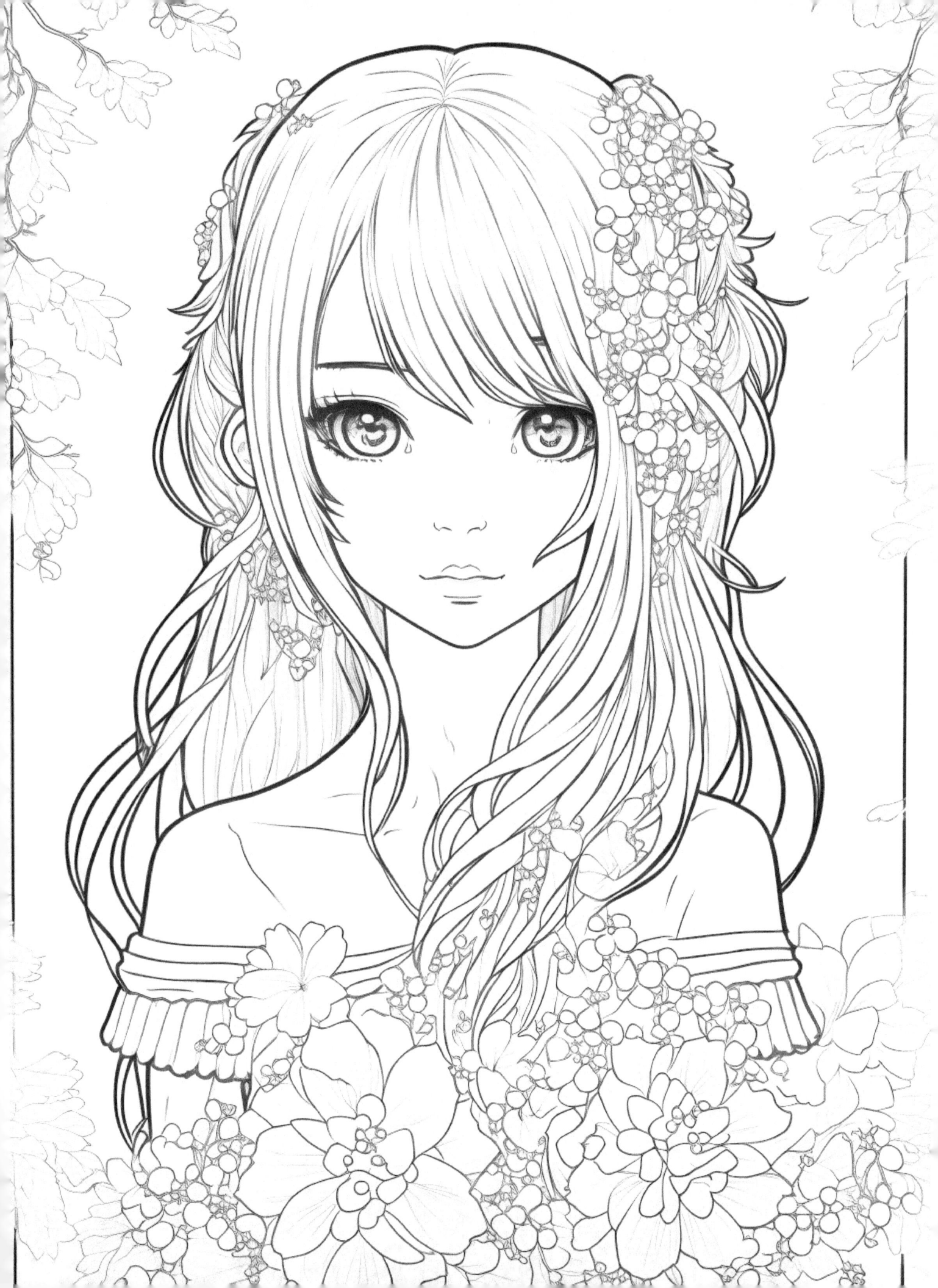

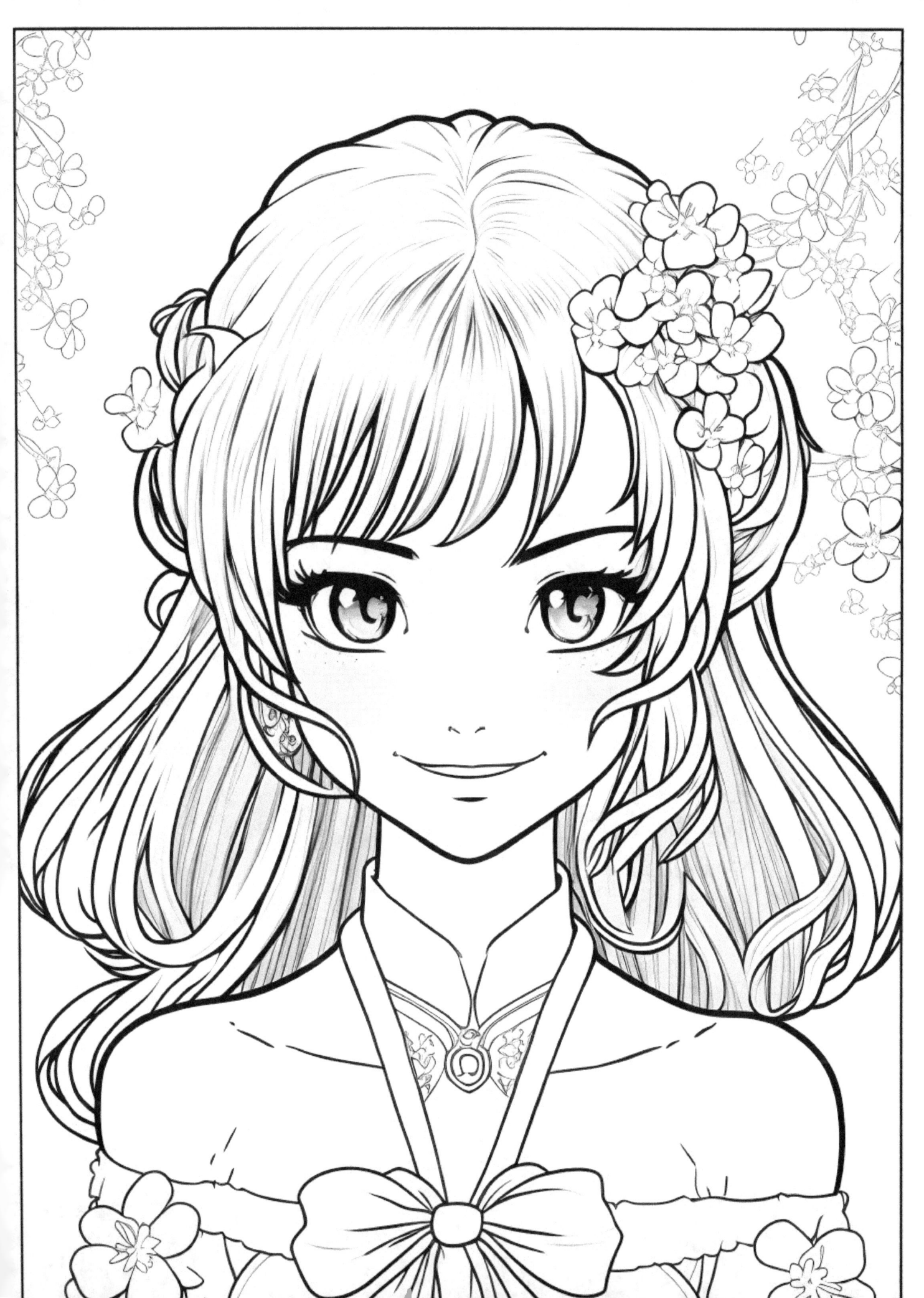

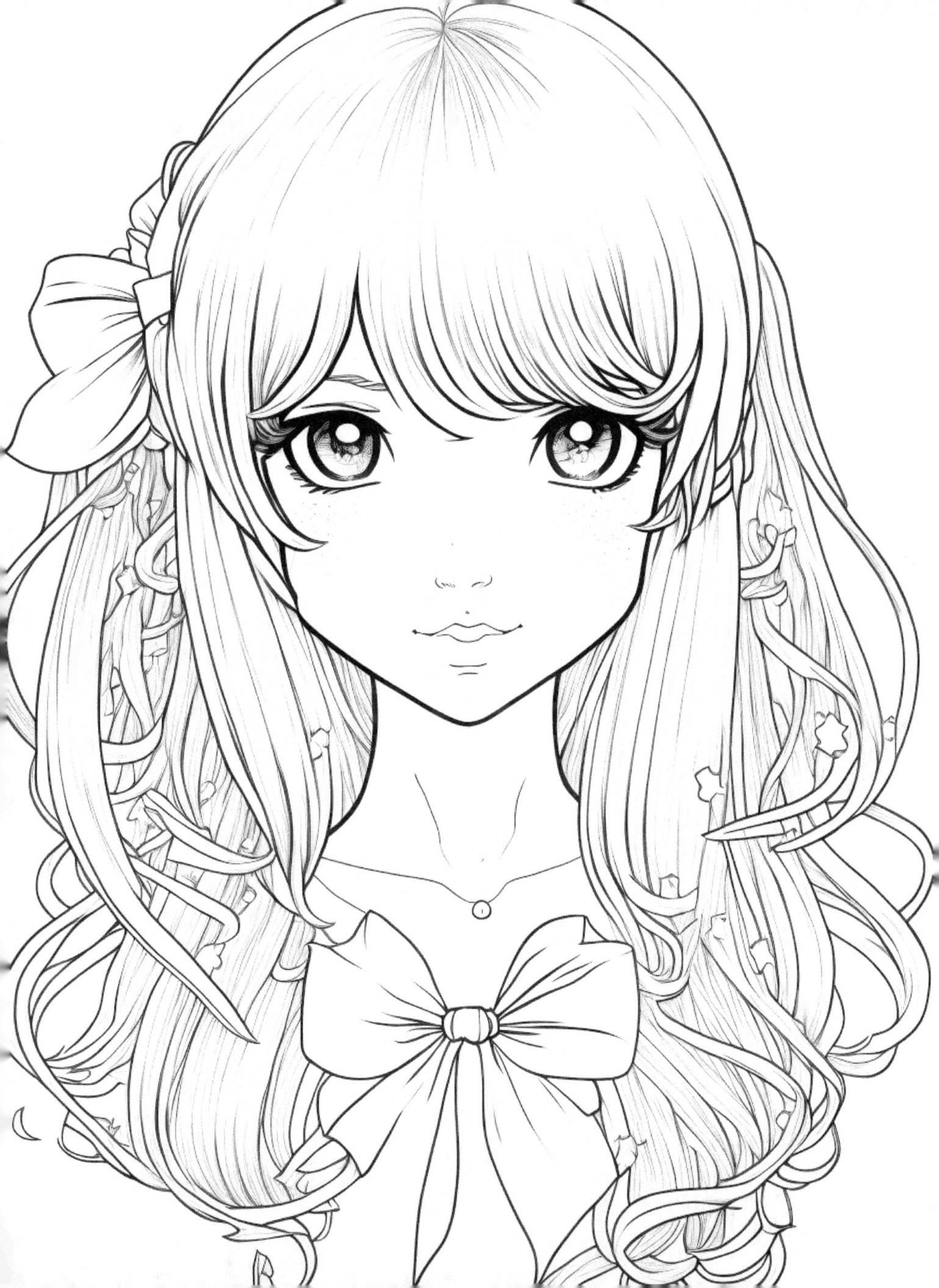

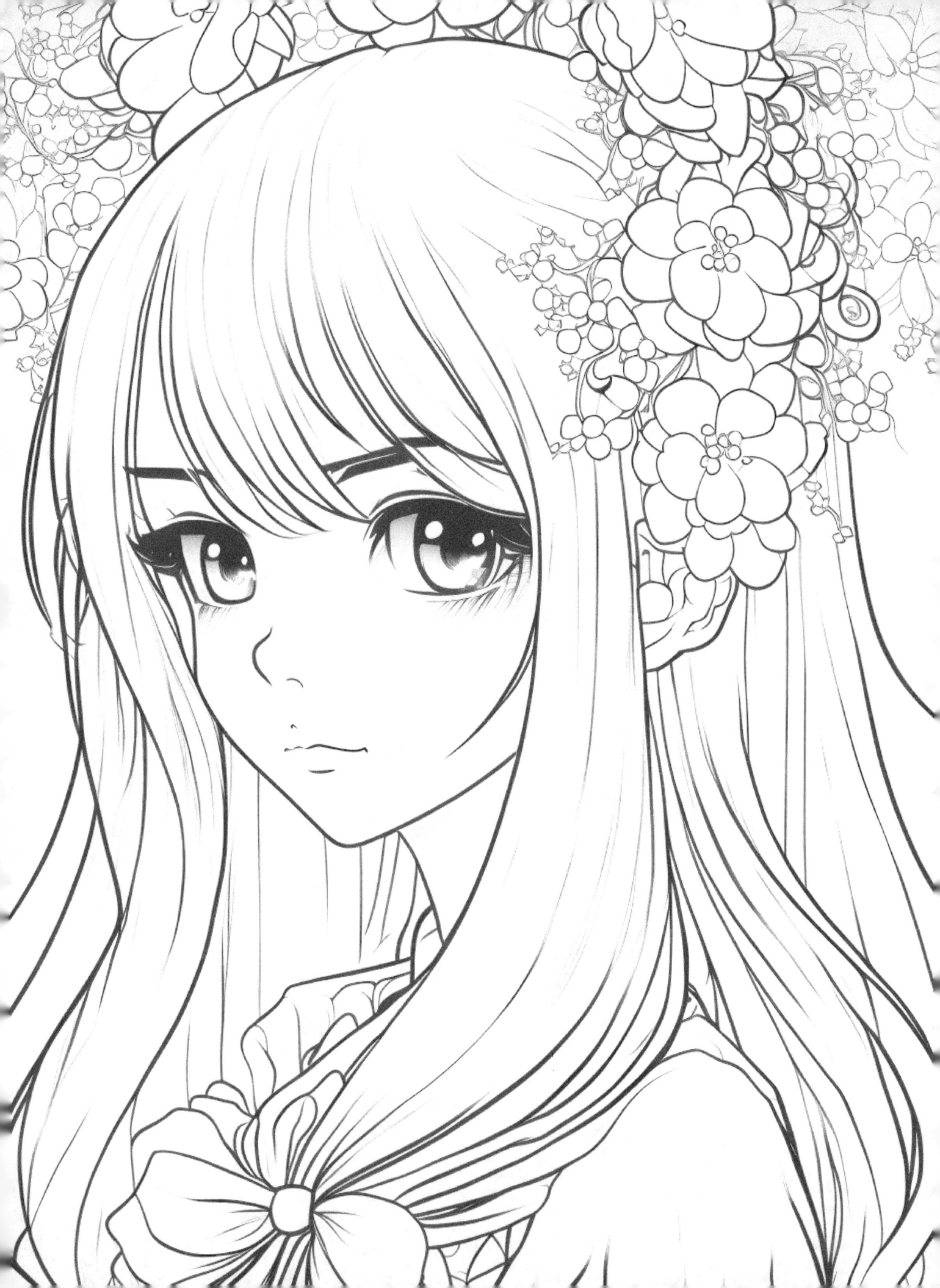

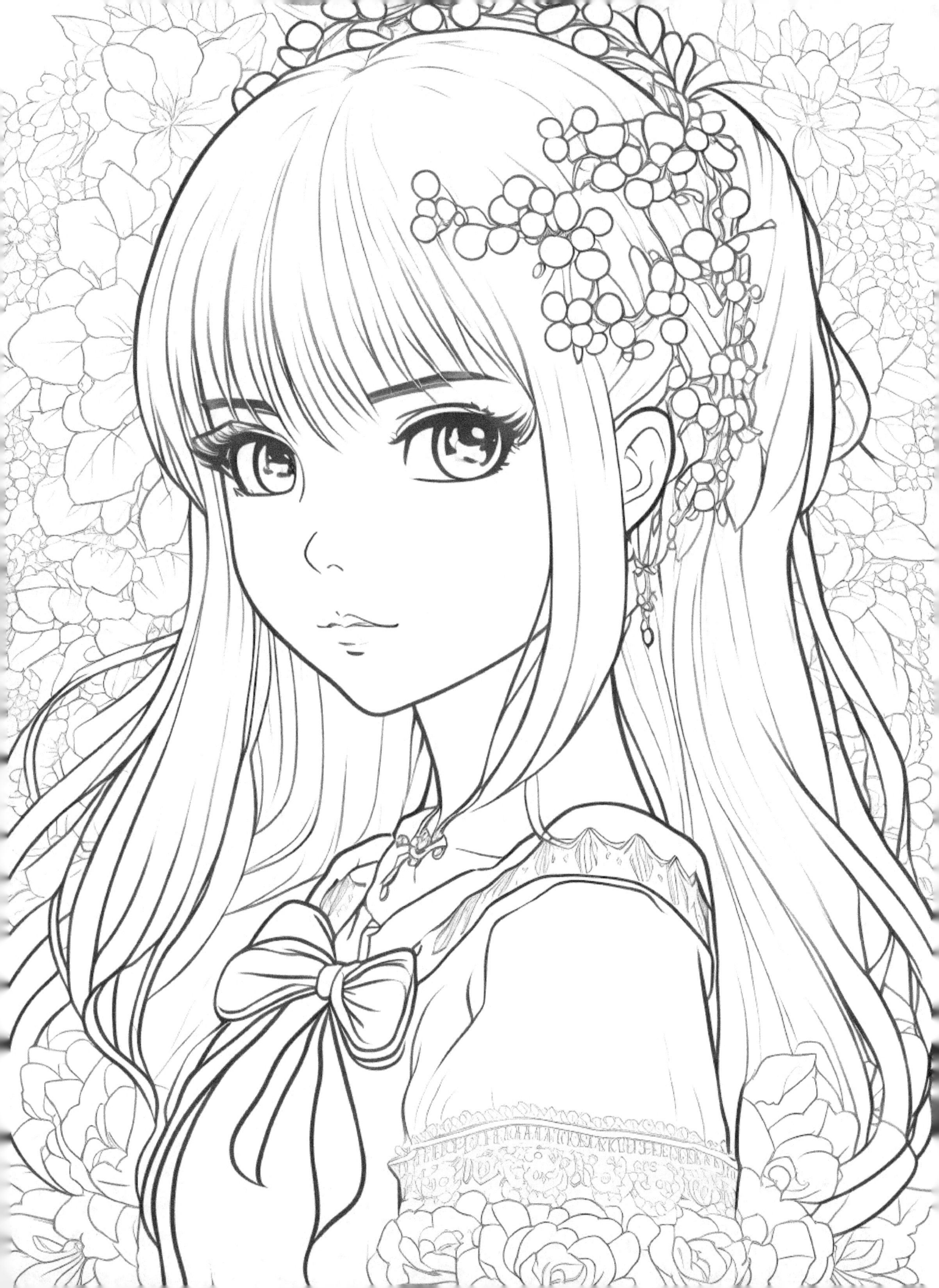

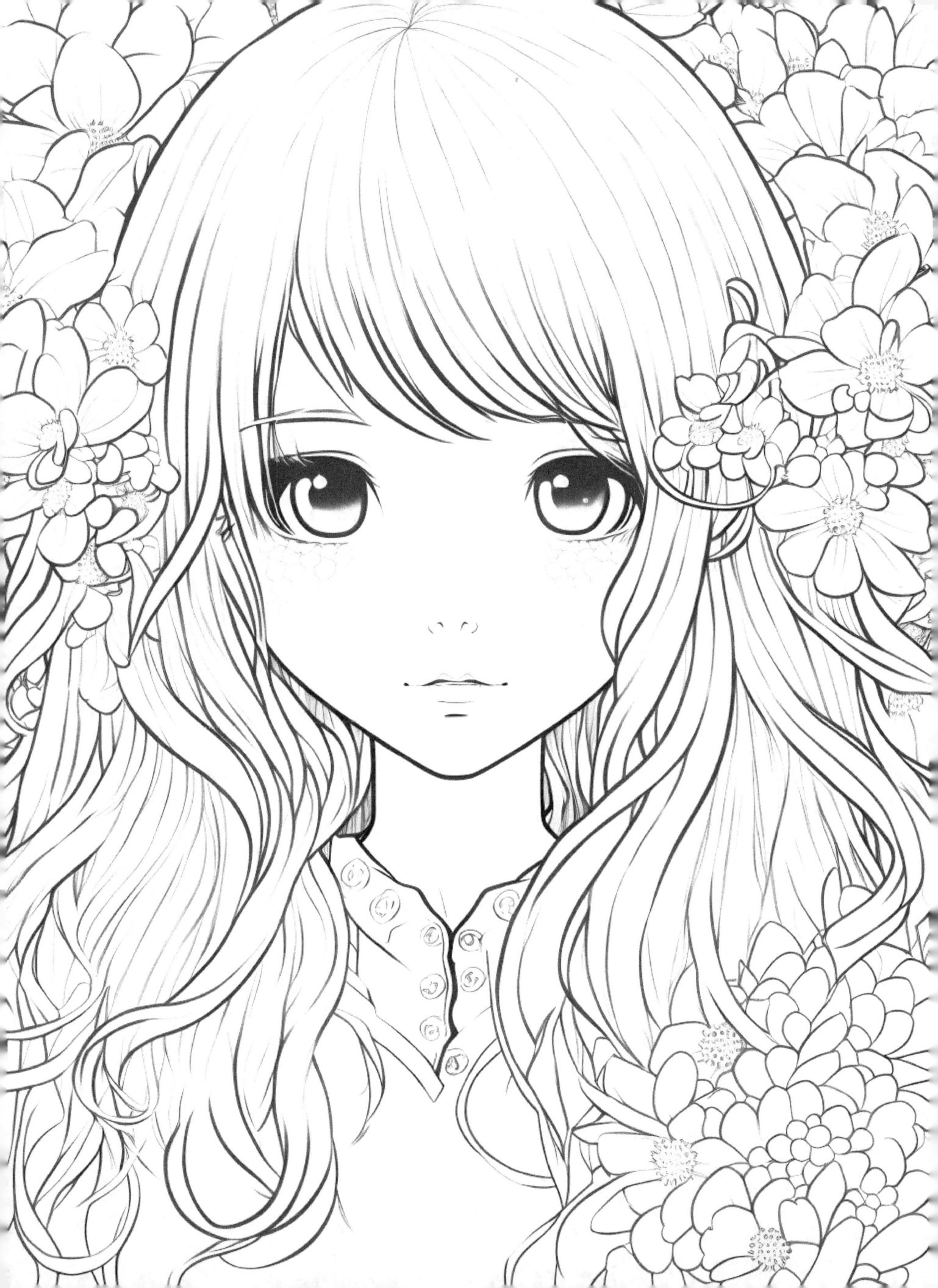

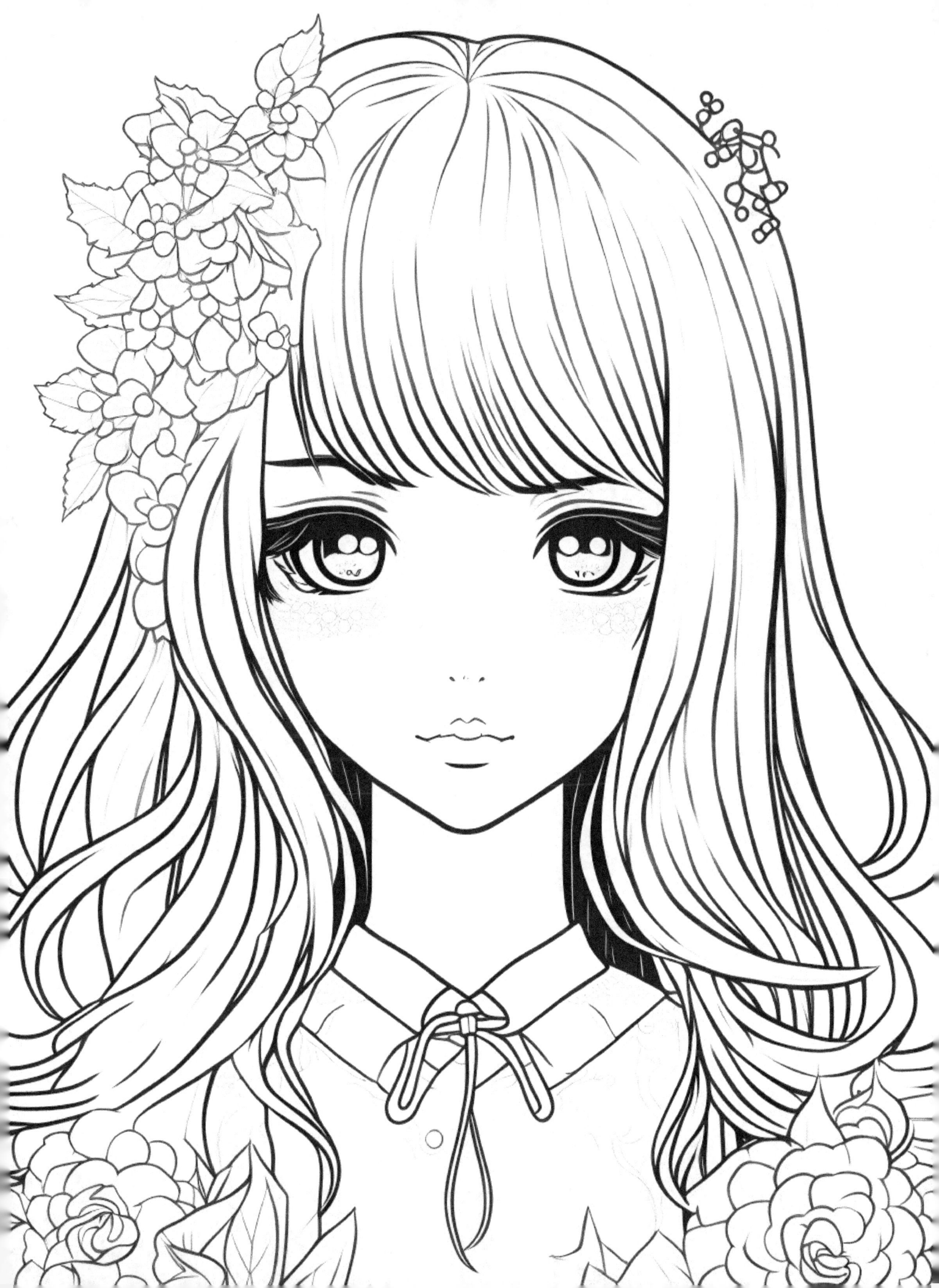

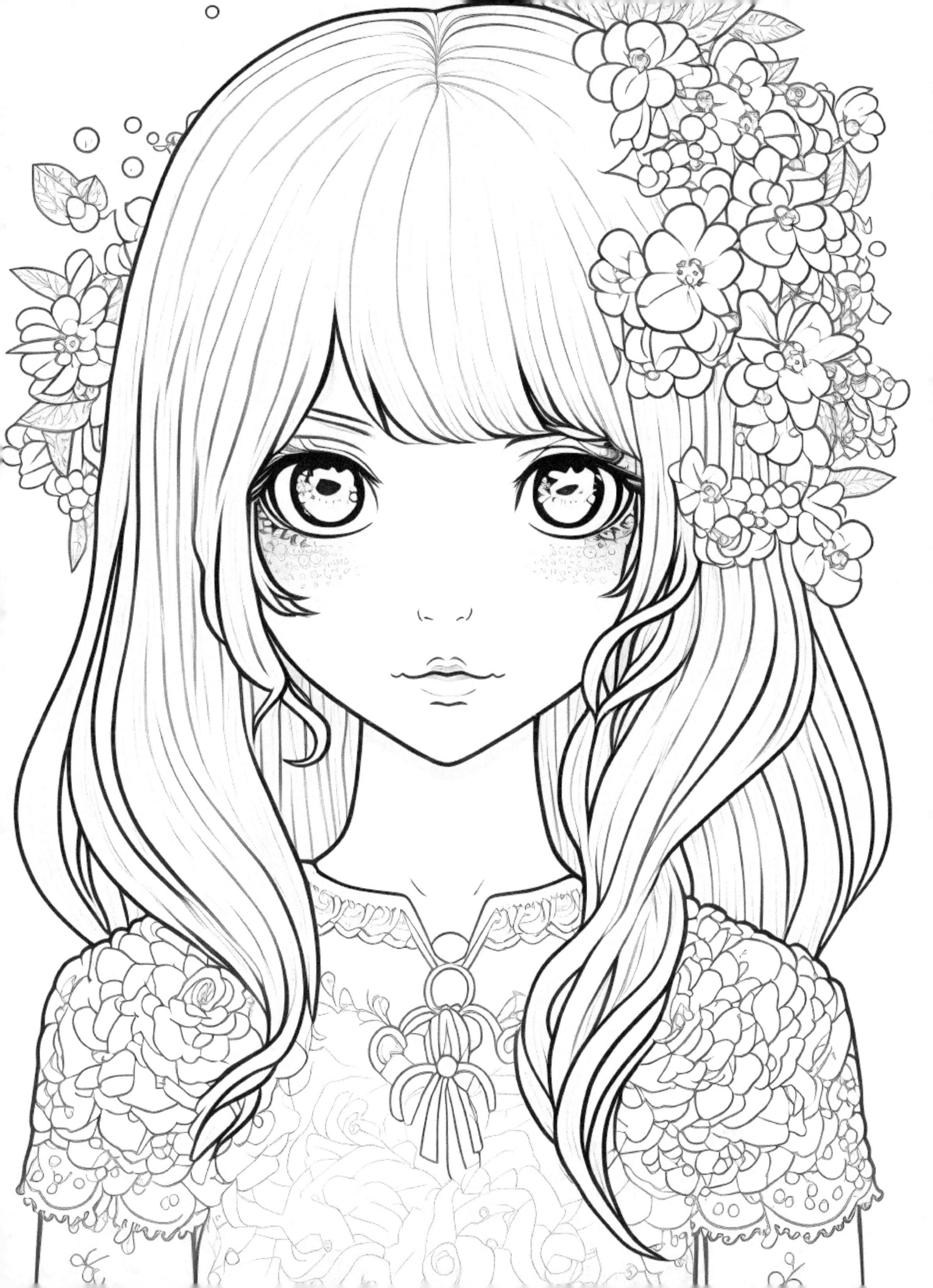

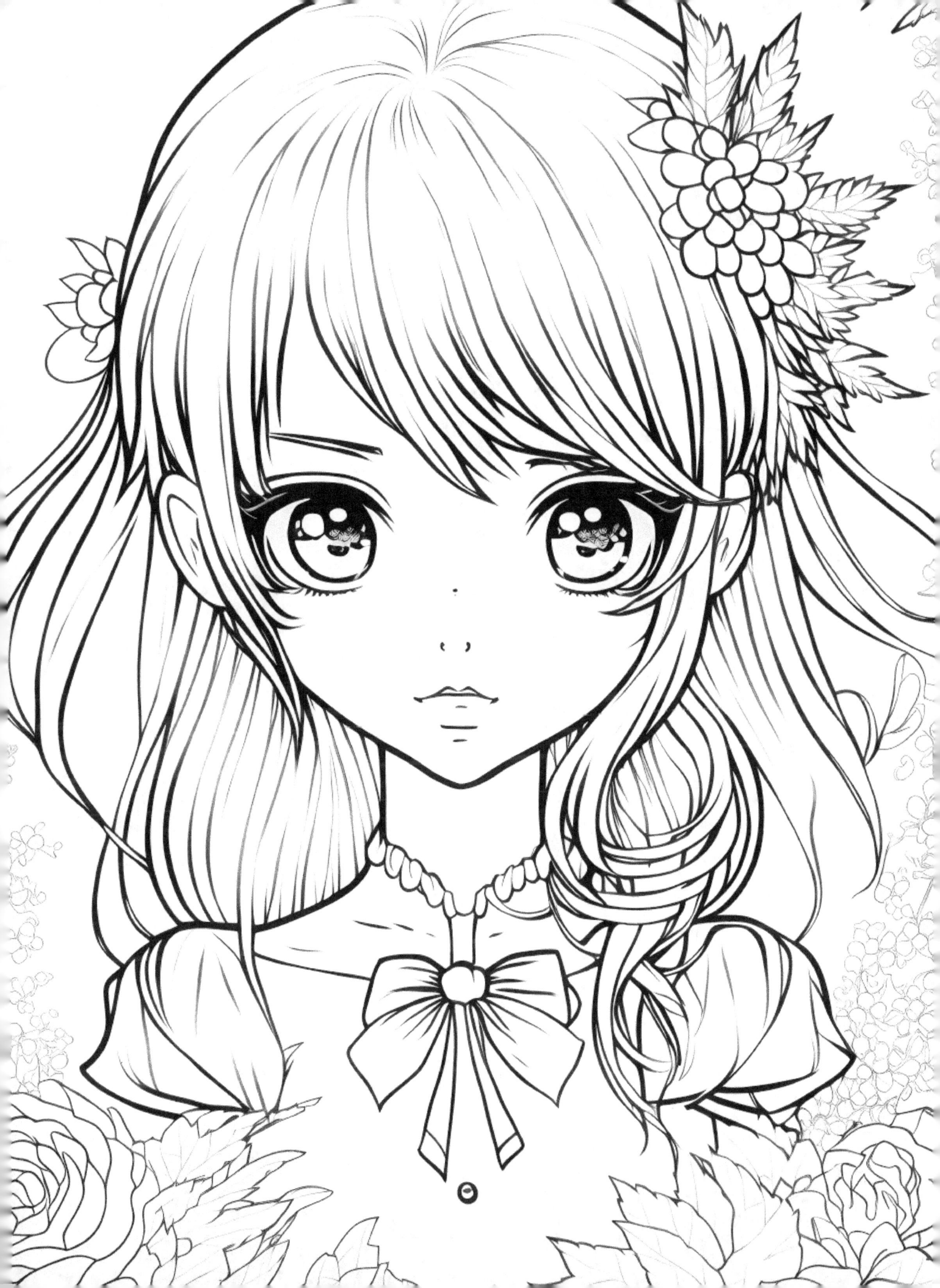

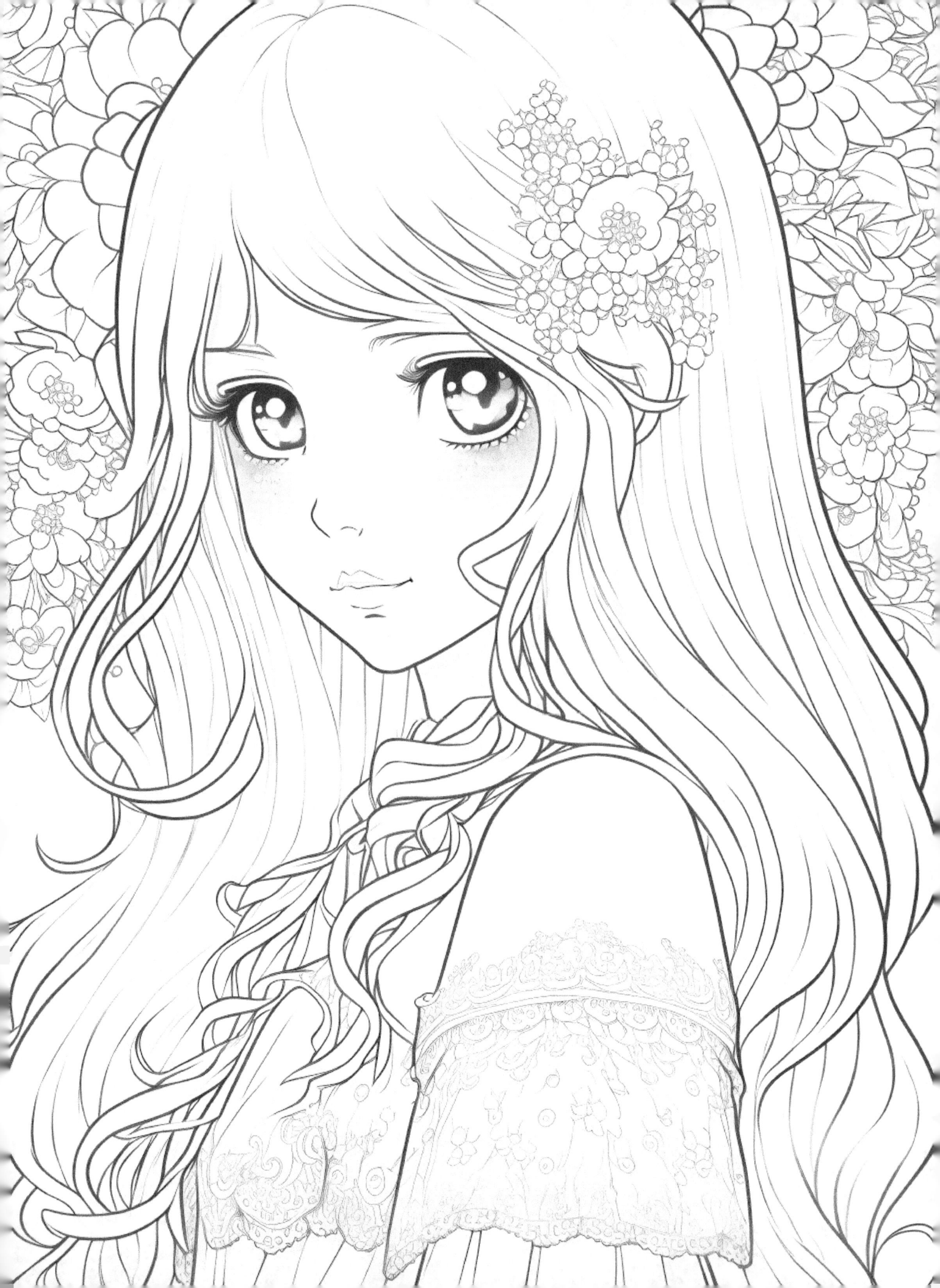

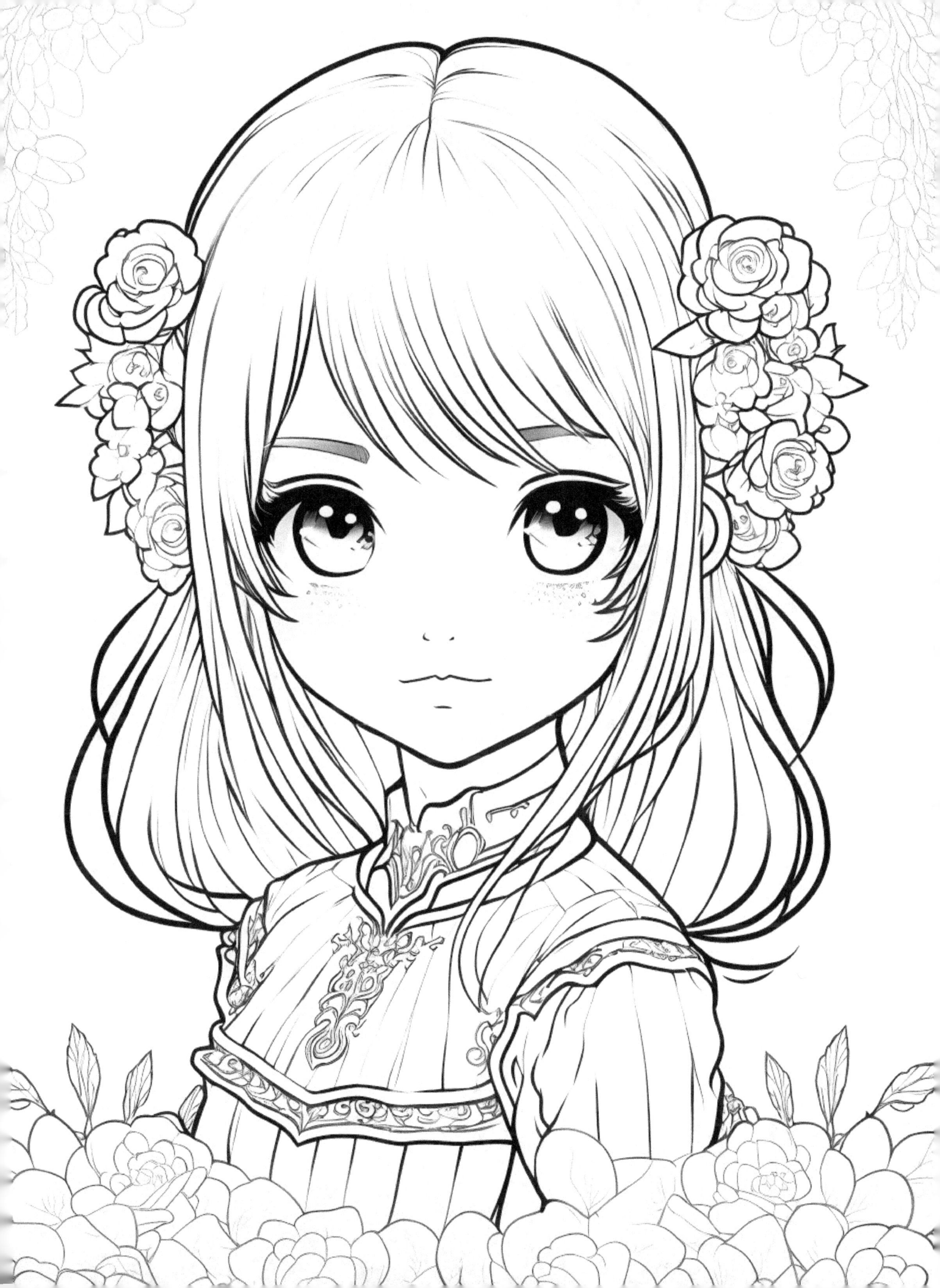

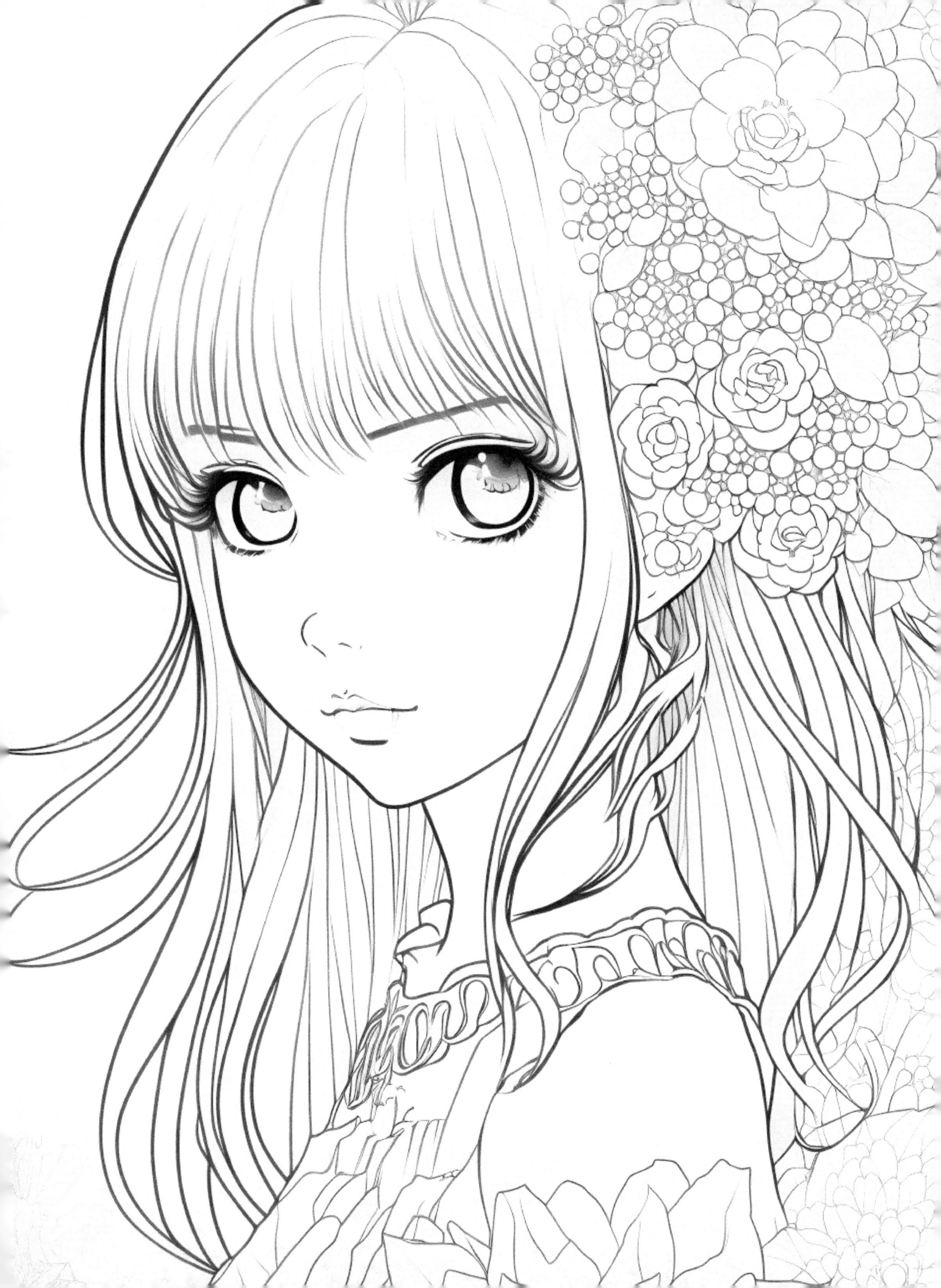

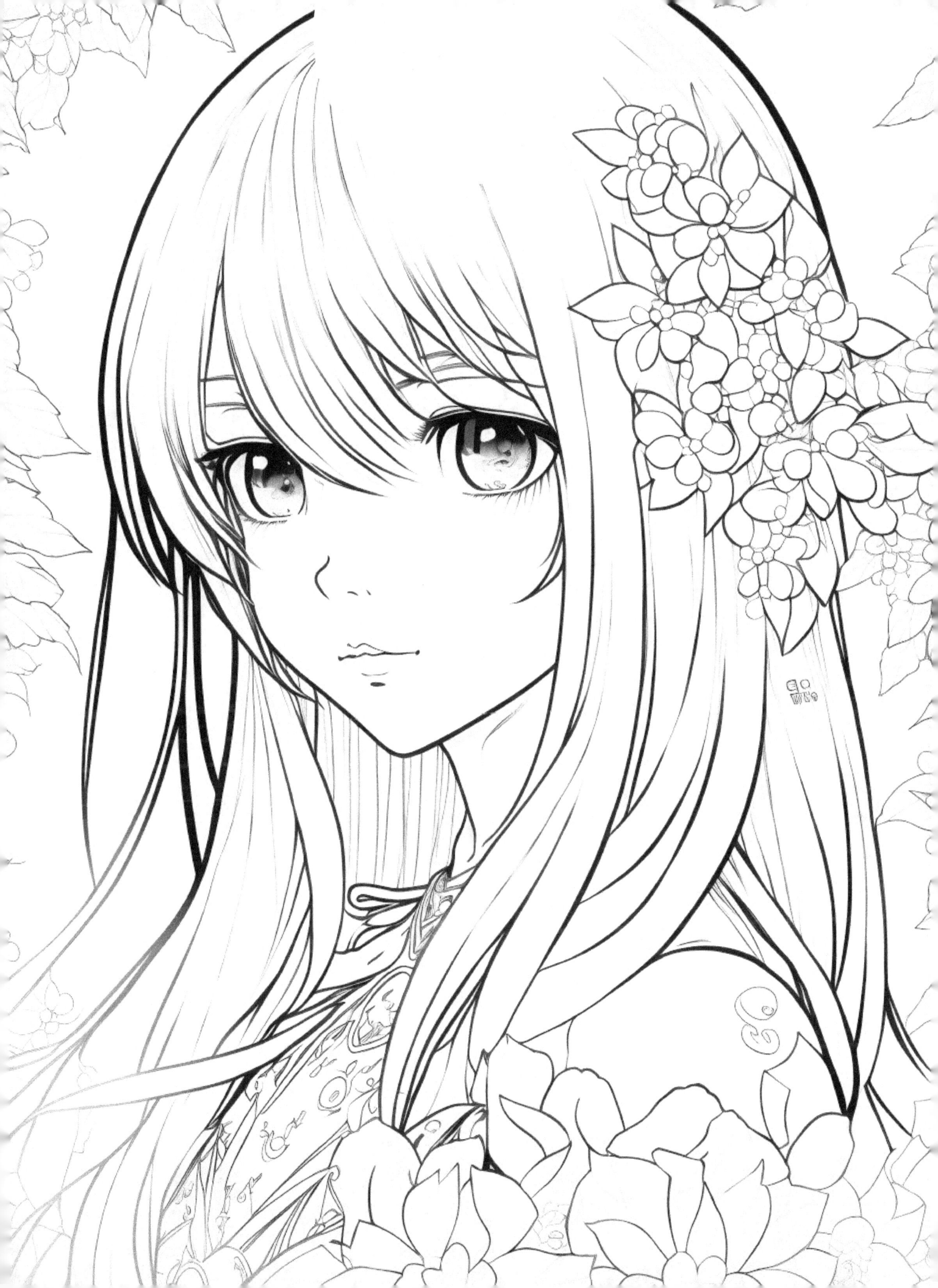

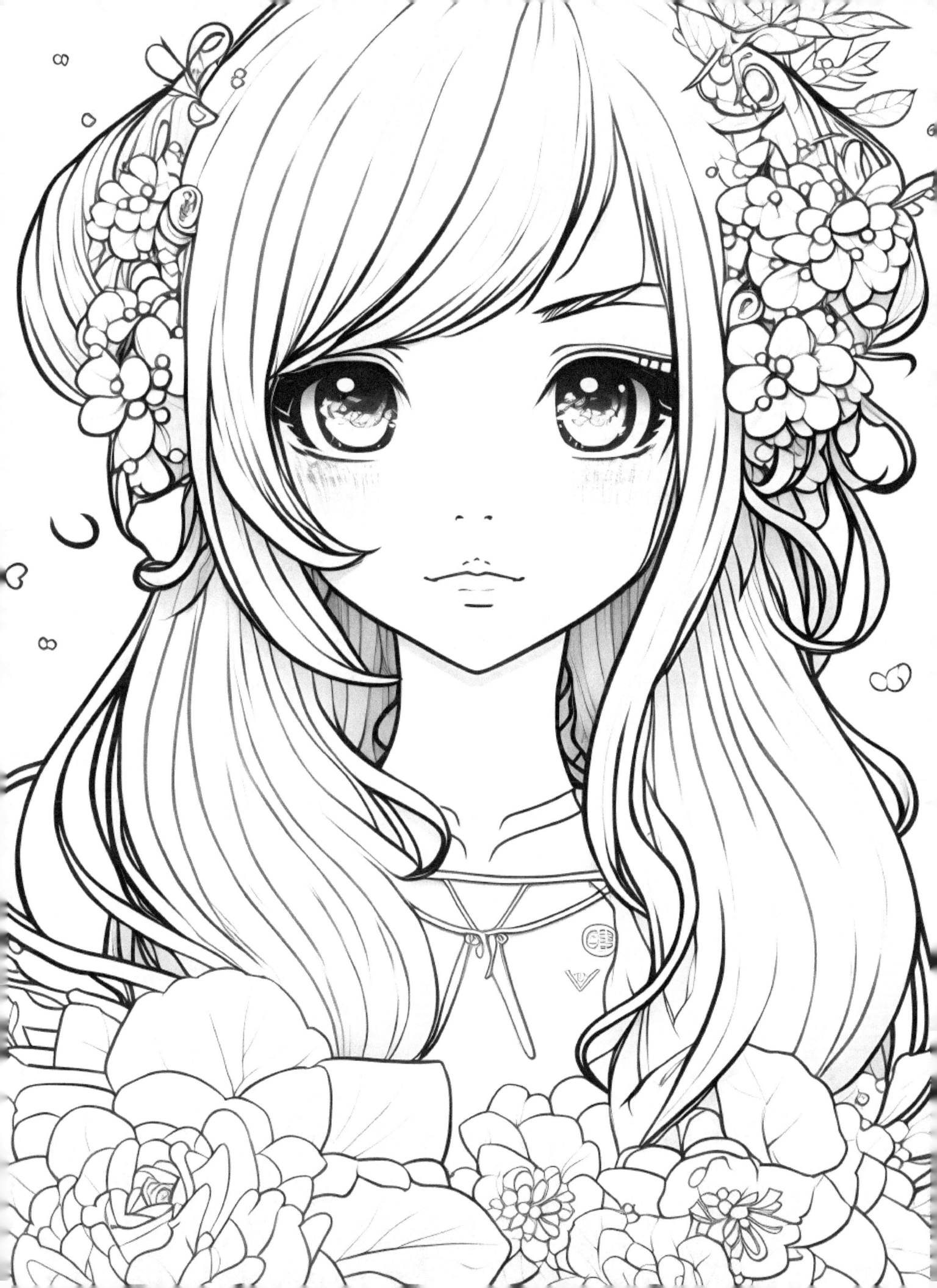

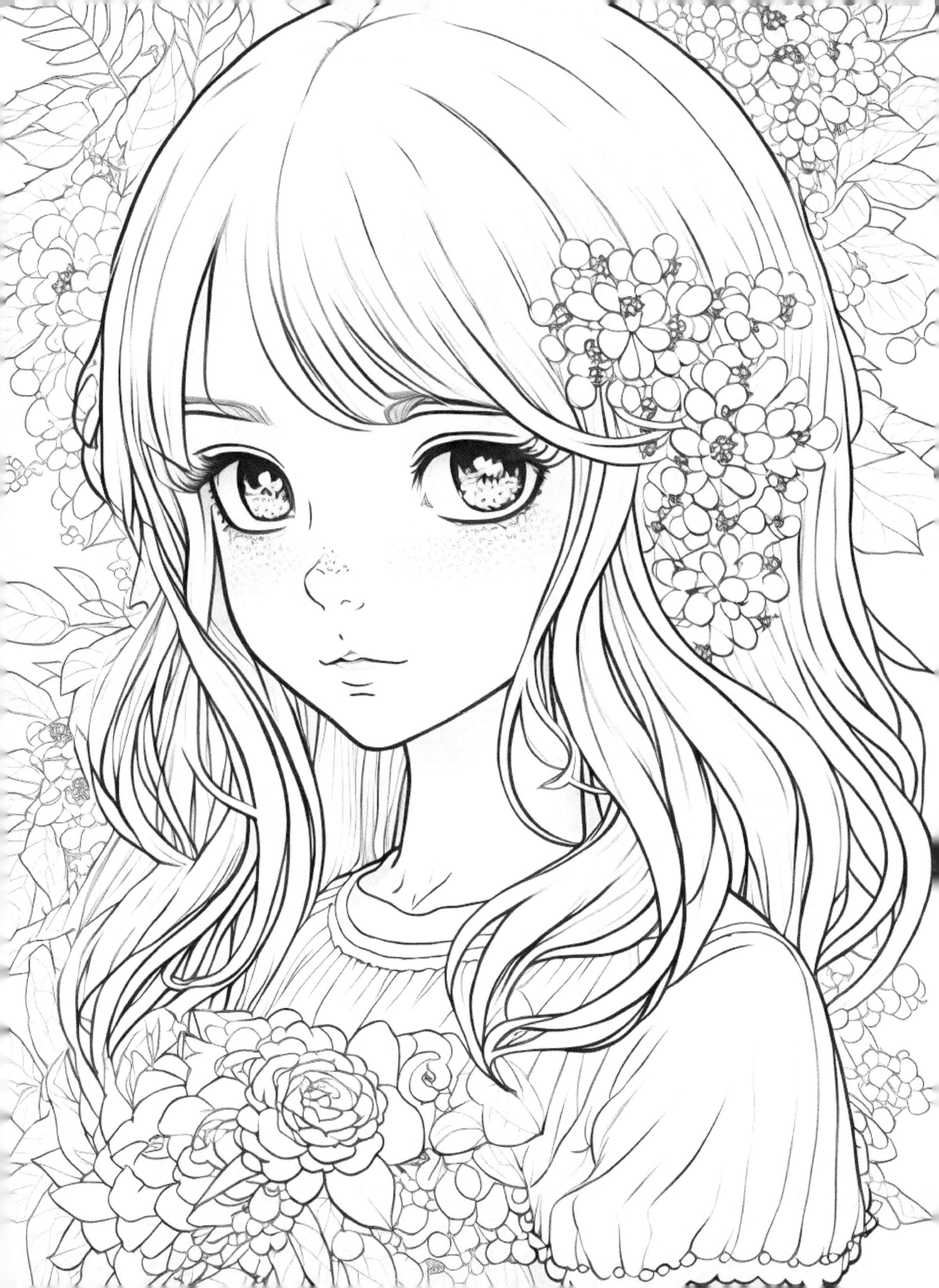

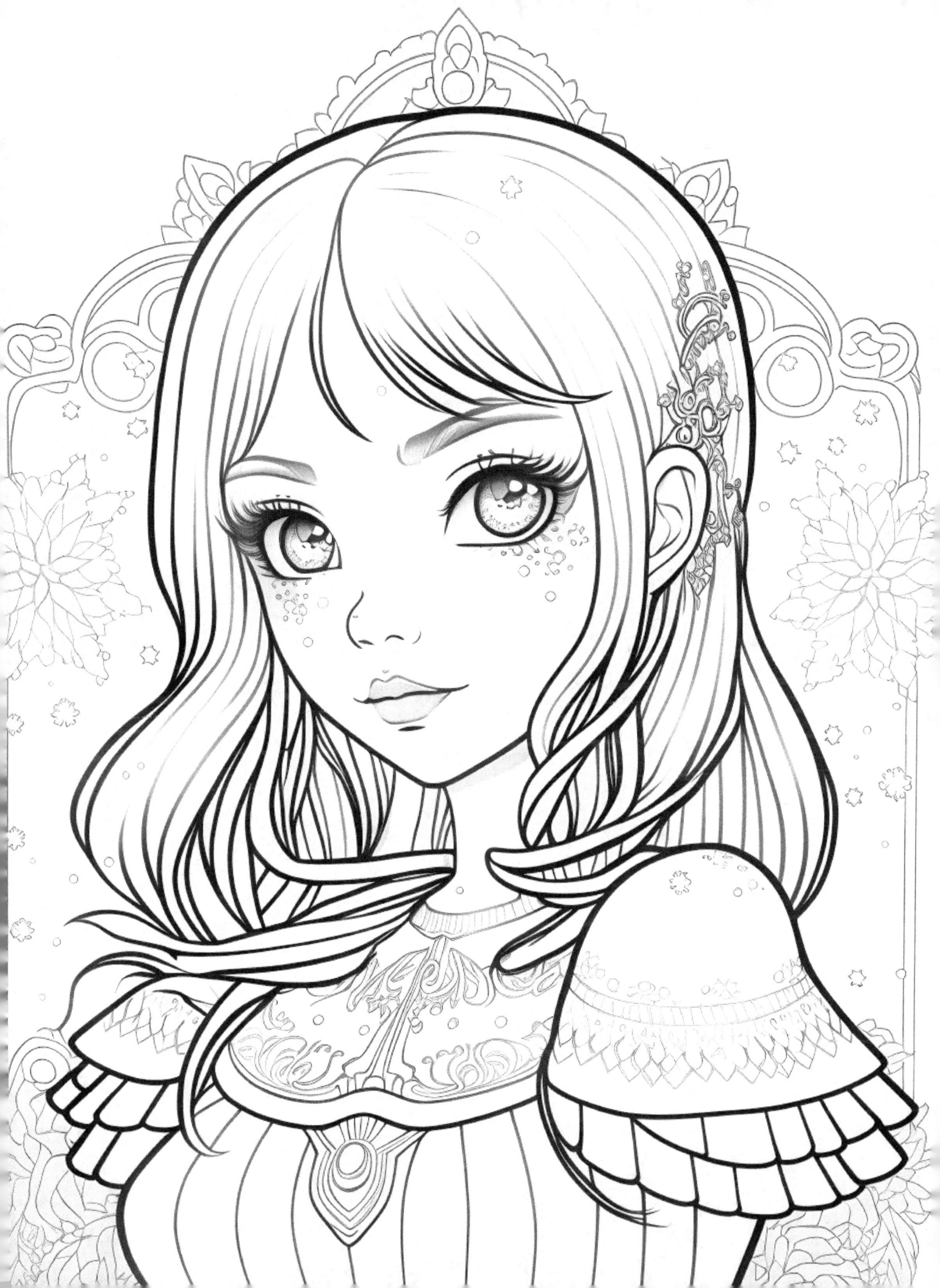

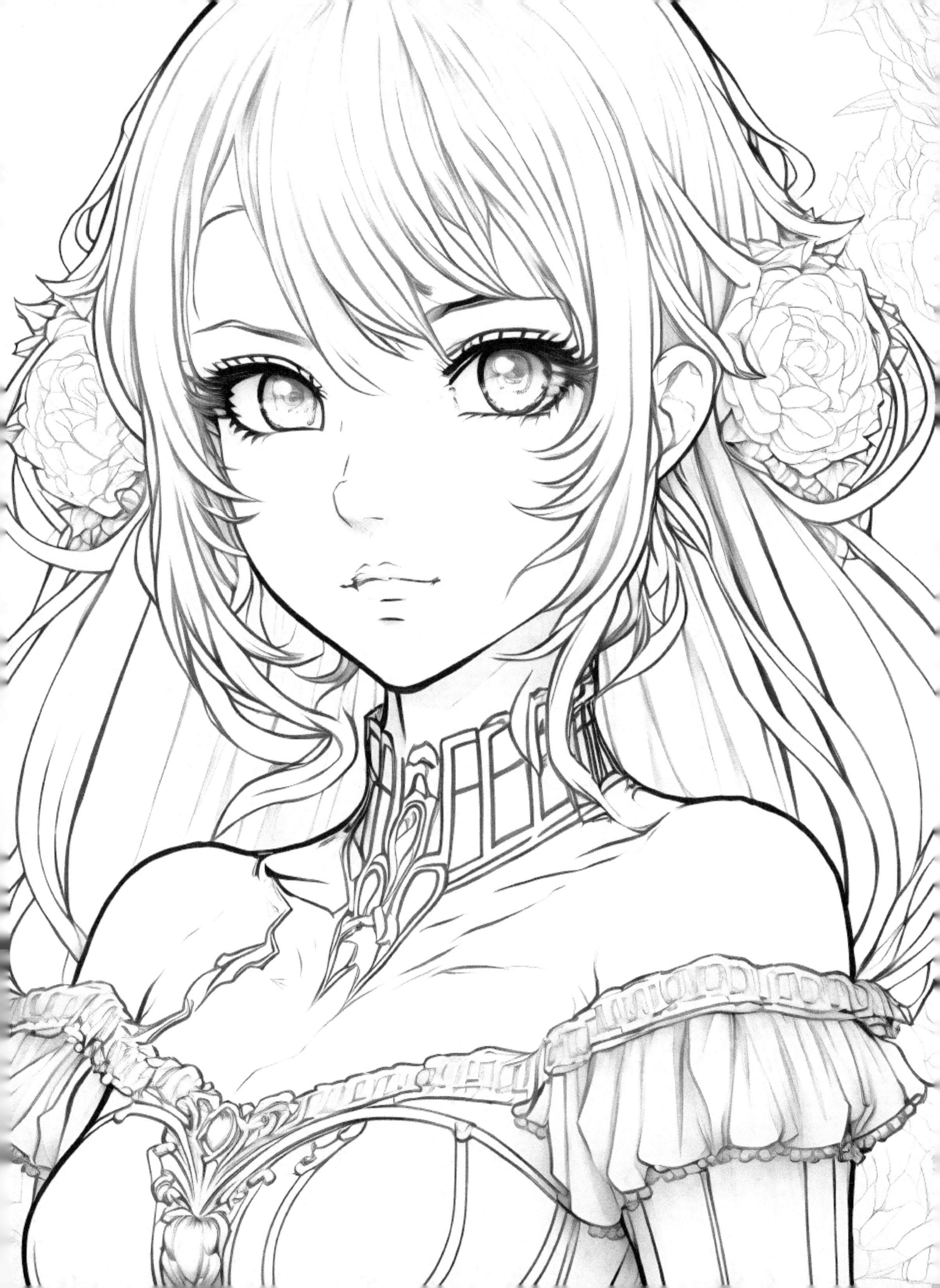

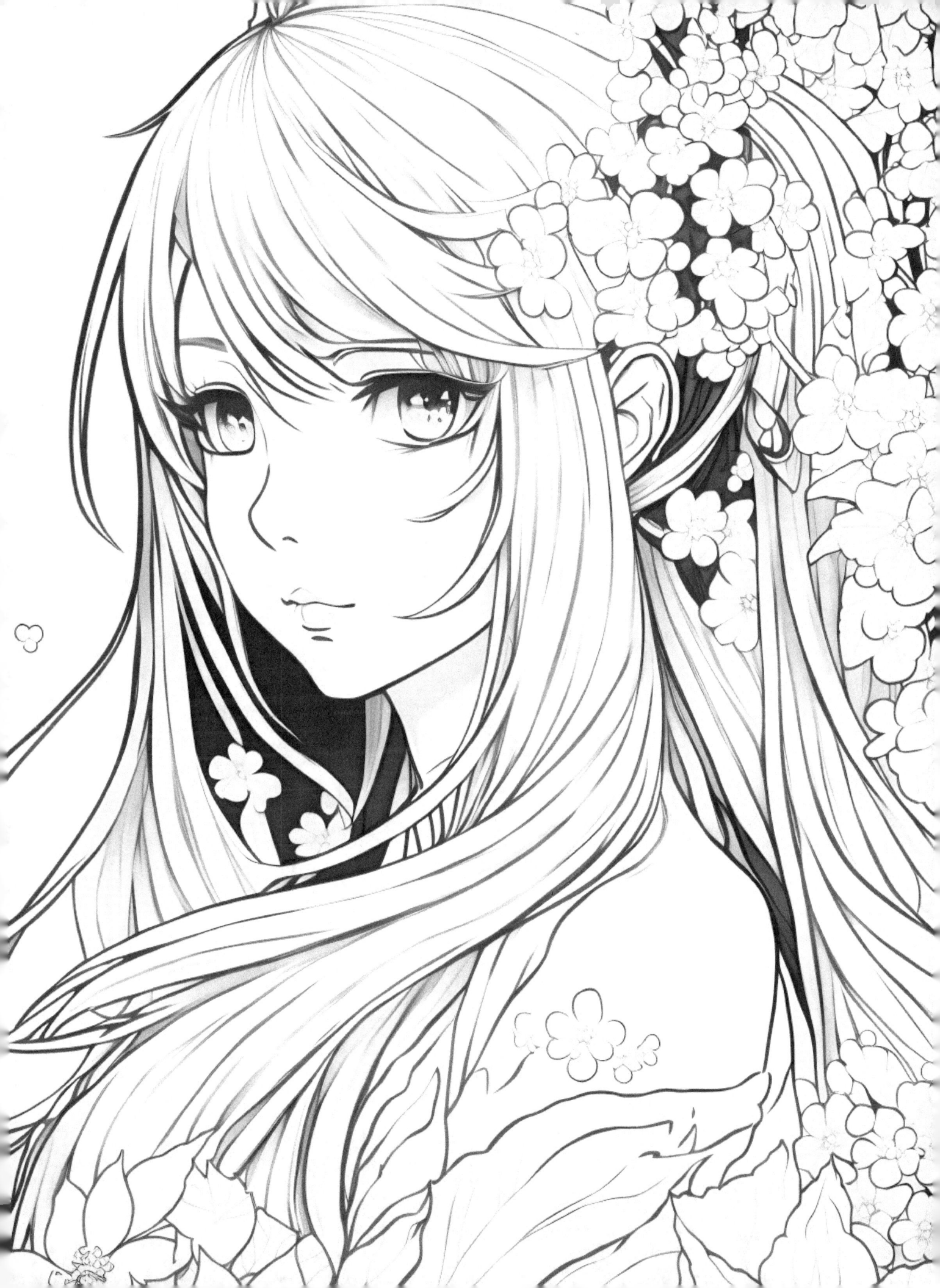

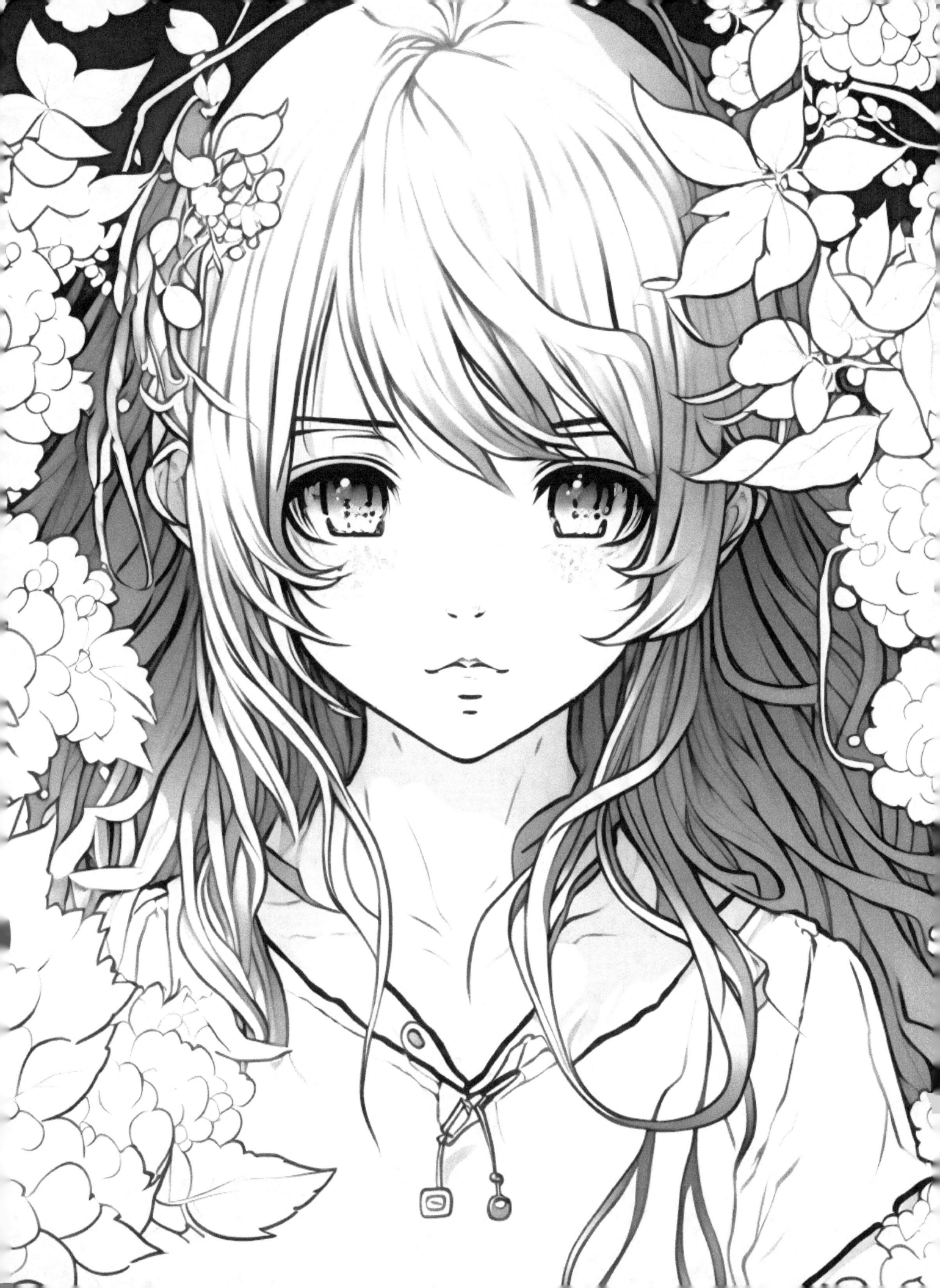

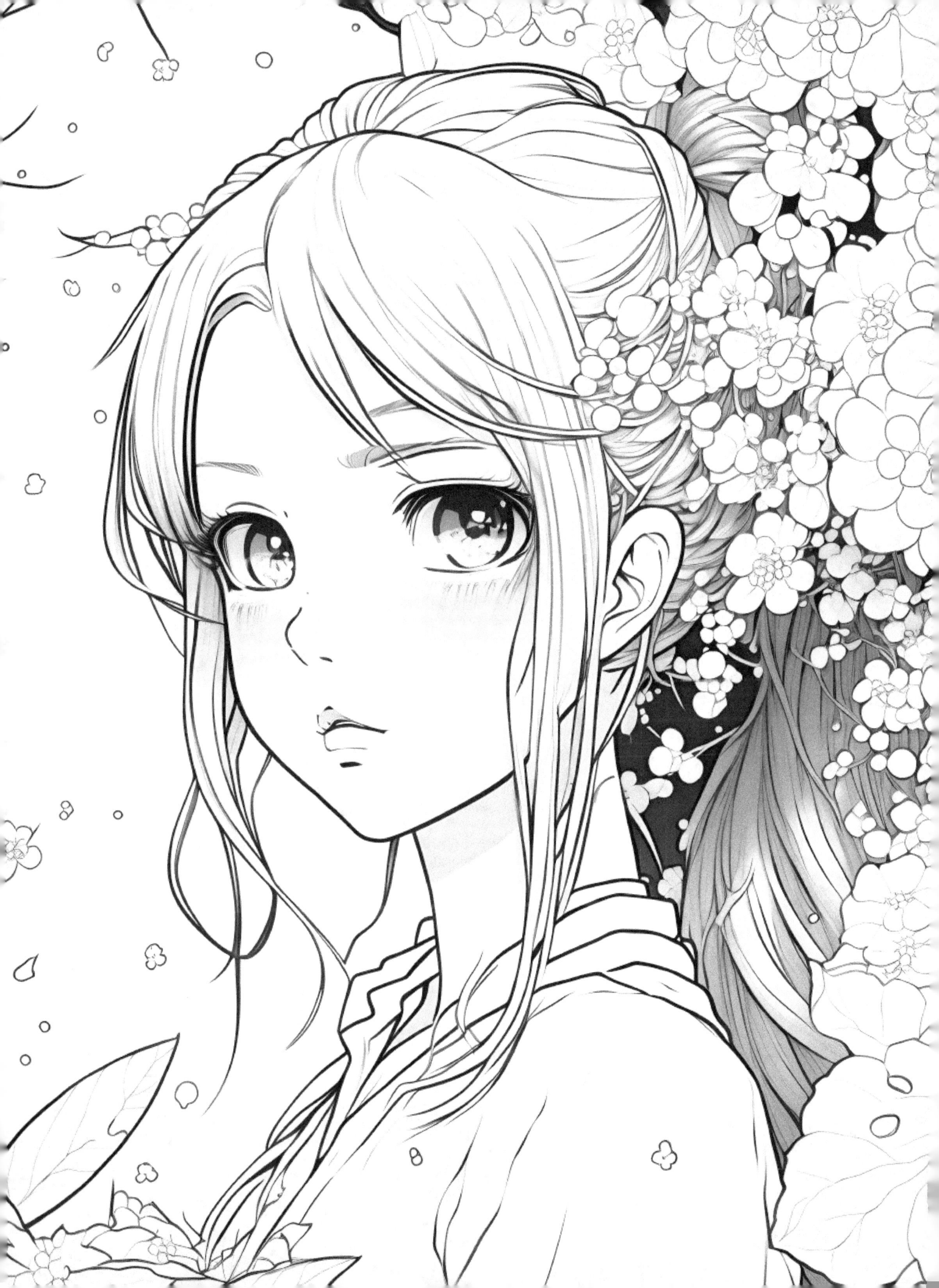

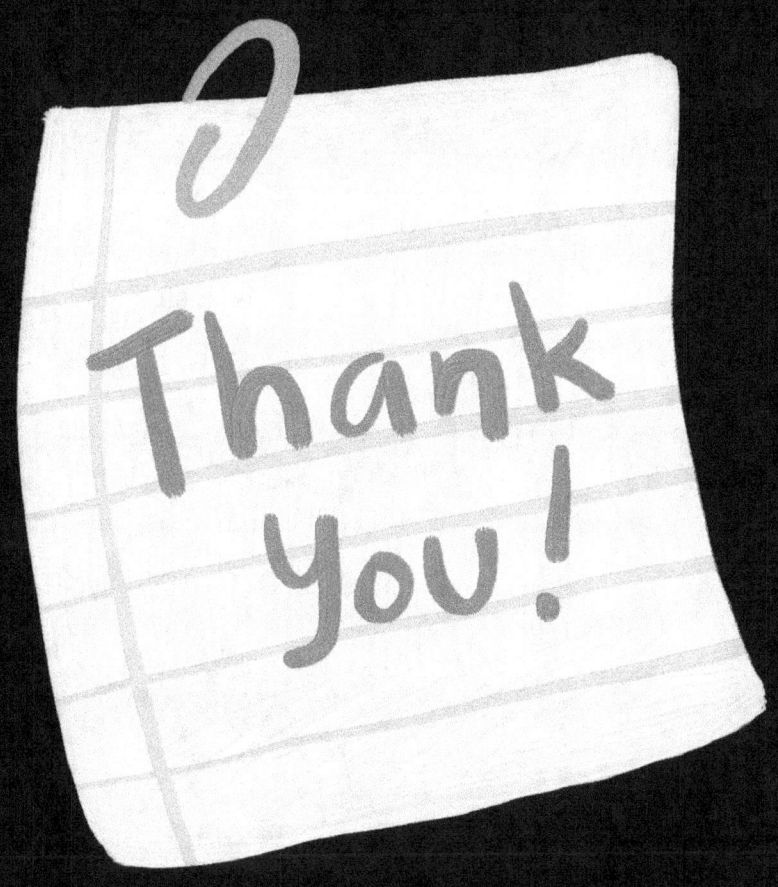

塗 SUPER
り KAWAII
絵 PRINCESSES

CAPI
CAMP
ESTUDIOS

www.ingramcontent.com/pod-product-compliance
Lightning Source LLC
Chambersburg PA
CBHW081626220526
45467CB00029B/3170